Living in the Raw Gourmet

Rose Lee Calabro

Book Publishing Company
Summertown, Tennessee

To contact Rose Lee Calabro: phone 877-557-4711
e-mail: livingintheraw1@hotmail.com

Cover design: Warren Jefferson
Photography: Warren Jefferson
Interior design: Gwynelle Dismukes

Published in the United States by
Book Publishing Company
P.O. Box 99
Summertown, TN 38483
1-888-260-8458

Printed in Canada

ISBN-13 978-1-57067-176-0
ISBN-10 1-57067-176-1

10 09 08 07 06 05   6 5 4 3 2 1

Calabro, Rose Lee.
  Living in the raw gourmet / by Rose Lee Calabro.
     p. cm.
  Includes index.
  ISBN-13: 978-1-57067-176-0
  ISBN-10: 1-57067-176-1
  1. Cookery (Natural foods) 2. Raw food diet. 3. Vegetarian cookery. I. Title.

TX741.C32 2005
641.5'63—dc22

2005013544

Recipes featured on the cover:
  Chiles Rellenos, p. 216
  Cheesecake with Fruit Topping, p. 248
  Mushroom Burger, p. 233

Some images © www.clipart.com

Dedication

I dedicate this book to my Mother, who was as wonderful in the physical as she is now.

Mother

I was nourished by your strength and positive attitude.

I was nurtured by the friendship we shared.

I was gifted by your timeless love.

Because of her premature death from hearth failure, I was to learn about health and natural healing. The changes I made resulted in the regaining of my health, and the adoption of a life-enhancing lifestyle.

And………. MOM,

To let you know, in life your heart never ever failed.

Thank you, for giving me life and saving mine.

Acknowledgments

With God's blessings, guidance, and inspiration this book was created.
I would like to acknowledge and thank:

My children

I tried to be a guiding light for both of you—I hope I succeeded. You both brought me incredible pride and joy. Motherhood could never have been more of an honor.

Keith Adams (my son)

The muse addressed you and you listened. I marvel at your multitude of talents and your ability to be a wild and creative spirit. You reached into your soul, recognized yourself, and expressed it artistically. What a gift you are to me and others!
I love you.

Kerrie Adams (my daughter)

Yours is the heart whose presence knows no bounds. Your inner light shines, offering others theirs. Your essence of true caring is the spiritual medication you administer to others for deep healing. You're everything I ever wanted to be.
I love you.

Gabriel Cousens, MD

Your inspired work has had a profound impact on the improvement of my health. I am extremely grateful to have you as a friend, doctor, and spiritual teacher. Thank you for your achievements, which have touched many lives, and your contributions toward saving the planet.

Judith Widell

I so appreciate the friendship, love, and support you have offered.
Thank you for your words of wisdom.

Contents

Foreword

Rose Lee Calabro's spirit would have passed off the planet if she had not discovered raw food nutrition in 1998. Rose Lee not only discovered, but took action on the magical rejuvenating powers of raw food. She discovered that raw food information is life-changing, life-extending, and life-friendly, and that it comes forth now as a karmic balance to the "anything goes" version of nutrition manipulated by giant food corporations and unconscious behavior.

Stop. Breathe. Check in with heart-centered action. With all the conflicting information on diet, what makes sense? Pesticides, herbicides, fungicides, larvicides, genetically modified organisms, chemical fertilizers, microwaves, pasteurization, homogenization, hormonally injected animals, color dyes, artificial additives, and high fructose corn syrup? Or raw, organic, sun-ripened plant food?

Raw plant food nutrition is the basis of all nutrition. It is the easiest food to procure without tools, fire, or technology. It is the food that is most conducive to and subconsciously connected to health. It is the food that is the most fun to eat (what is more fun than eating a mango with your lover?), and is the type of food that is most closely associated with our picture of paradise (drinking a coconut on the beach).

Raw food diets are the only diets found in nature. Raw food nutrition is in alignment with the original design of life—the "Creator's Original Intent." With all the talk about spirituality and religion filling thousands of books with esoteric ideas, the most obvious "spiritual" discipline is often overlooked, which is eating from Mother Nature directly. This is direct access to God. This is direct access to spirituality. Microwaving, boiling, frying, burning, pasteurizing, and cooking disassociates us from a spiritual connection with the Creator.

Even though it may be boiled to death or cooked into oblivion, everyone still knows that Mom's home cooking tastes better and is more nourishing than other food. That is because Mom's food has love in it. Loving our food is perhaps the key to unlocking all nutritional disorders worldwide. The mass consumption of food grown, raised, shipped, and prepared without consciousness or love is yet another major reason why humanity has become estranged from a real spiritual connection with creation. If we were to love enough we would do our best to leave all living animals, especially conscious animals, alone and do our best to stay on a plant-based diet.

Based on Dr. Masaru Emoto's work in his books *The Messages of Water* (volumes 1–3), we now know scientifically that water responds to our consciousness and that messages of love are instantaneously reflected in the structure of water nearby. This seems to be the reason why raw, water-rich plant foods are capable of carrying love vibrations better than any other type of food. Cooked food has lost its water content.

Rose Lee and I come from a place in our hearts where we believe this approach to nutrition is something that we get to do, not something we have to do. We have been given, by grace, the opportunity to celebrate in this type of nutrition. Through grace, we have been provided, and can provide, information on how to eat food that makes us feel truly phenomenal each moment. Our diet allows us to experience every day as the best day ever!

Through our discovery and incorporation of raw food nutrition into our lifestyles, we have become aware of a new type of freedom available to all of us. Food is about freedom of choice. Real choices. Unique choices. Being able to select more options when you click down the computer screen of life. America has always been and will always be the land of opportunity: the place where freedom of choice is available. That is why people are climbing over walls, jumping on ships, and hiding in trucks to get into America. Just as we have the most absurd food choices available, we also have the greatest, most health-enhancing foods ever grown in the history of the world.

Should you consider adding raw food nutrition into your lifestyle? Consider this: if you desire the same results you have always had, please, do the same thing you have always done. If you want something different in this life, you must be doing something different every day. Changing your diet by adding in mineral-rich, organic plant foods can radically shift the direction of your life, your health, your joy, and your destiny.

Consider the words of Marcus Aurelius Antoninus, Roman philosopher and emperor: "Is anyone afraid of change? Why, what can take place without change? What then is more pleasing to the universal nature? And canst thou take a bath unless the wood undergoes a change? And canst thou be nourished unless the food undergoes a change? And can anything else that is useful be accomplished without change? Dost thou not see then that for thyself also to undergo change is just the same, and equally necessary for the universal nature?"

As we move forward with our dietary transformation, it is important to have the power of distinctions without judgments. Judgments destroy the diversity of life, because they indicate an emotional attachment, whereas the power of distinction allows us to intelligently and wisely navigate the myriad of choices before us without getting emotionally involved. If we judge other people because of their food choices, then they, consciously or subconsciously, pick up on our feelings and begin to judge us or not want to be around us. However, if we make wise and intelligent choices based on distinctions, then people will naturally gravitate toward us and want to know why we are making the choices we are making—they will feel attracted instead of repulsed.

How do we crack the code on transforming our diet? Simply by adding new raw food items into our diet. Have fresh fruit for snacks, add salads to lunch and dinner, make the salad your meal, create the wonderful recipes shared in this book. Simple things. This, in effect, crowds out other choices and clues us into and sensitizes us to those foods that really make us feel good and energized after eating them. It makes the process enjoyable and easy.

What to eat? Fruits, vegetables, nuts, seeds, seaweeds, sprouts, wheatgrass, herbs, fermented foods (sauerkraut, kimchee, etc.), superfoods (aloe vera, spirulina, blue-green algae, chlorella, bee pollen, maca, cacao beans, goji berries, etc.), and many wonderful condiments (discussed in this book) can be added to our diet. All these wonderful foods can be combined together with love to create the most fantastic cuisine ever. That is the magic you will find in these pages.

Enjoy in joy!

—David Wolfe, JD, raw foodist since 1994, CEO of www.rawfood.com, author of *Eating for Beauty, The Sunfood Diet Success System,* and *Naked Chocolate.*

Introduction
WHAT IS LIVING FOOD?

The first questions that inevitably come up as I talk with people about incorporating more living and raw food into their diets are What exactly is living food? and Why are living and raw food better than processed food? These are excellent questions, both of which I had when I first became aware that there is something called living food.

As I quickly learned, the best answers to these questions come through experiencing living food directly. There was no doubt in my mind after eating this food exclusively for just one month that it provided my body and mind with something no other food or diet has ever given me.

I now realize that compared to all other foods living food is the superstar. When living food is added to any meal (especially one that is at least 50 percent raw), it adds a new dimension to the meal's nutritional value—namely, an extraordinary ability to heal the body and mind.

The easiest way to recognize a living food is to answer this question: Is it still growing? If your response is yes, then you know it's a living food. Good examples of living food are the vegetables and fruits growing in the wild or in your garden. My favorite memories of eating living food are the times I picked wild berries and ended up eating most of them before I got home, or the many occasions I was tempted to bite into a tomato or carrot that I had just picked from my garden. It's an incredible experience I call "from garden to mouth." If you've had similar experiences, you'll surely agree there is a distinct difference in the flavor and energy these foods provide.

If you were not fortunate enough to have grown up around a garden, today in our supermarkets you can find a new source of living food in the form of fresh sprouts and baby greens, which are alive and still growing as you "pick" them off the shelf. These young living plants can add valuable nutrition that may be missing from your meals. With this book you will learn how to prepare a new world of tasty living food you can grow and prepare right in your own kitchen using techniques that take minimum effort and result in fantastic health benefits.

Raw food is the other star of health and nutrition. Just remember that the older raw food is, the fewer nutrients it contains. When any living food is picked, it is separated from its life energy, its connection to Earth; its growth begins to slow. Within twenty-four to forty-eight hours after fresh produce is picked, all growth stops. This is when a living food becomes a mature raw food. As days go by, a raw food's powerful healing energies slowly begin to diminish. This may be evidenced by a change in appearance (for example, once vivid colors may become dull, skin may wrinkle, or dark areas may form), a soft or mushy texture, or a sweeter taste. Be aware of this and choose only the freshest raw produce when you shop.

On the rare occasions I find myself without living and raw food, every part of me misses them. This has happened at restaurants, where menu choices are typically limited to mostly cooked items, or long seminars, when only baked snacks and coffee are available during the short breaks. I notice now that within just an hour after eating a meal that doesn't contain enough living and raw food I feel tired and slightly achy and my mind is not as clear as I've become accustomed to. Sometimes it takes up to two days after I return to my regular diet to fully recover my "performing edge." I love feeling healthy and vibrant!

What I have learned about cooked food is that it has no healing energy. To demonstrate this, try planting two types of seeds, raw and roasted (or boiled, if you think they will have a better chance of growing). I guarantee that only one of these will grow, and that is the raw one, because it is the only one that contains a life force.

Nutritionally speaking, living food is the richest source of enzymes, oxygen, chlorophyll, vitamins, essential fatty acids, and fiber. It also contains the proper ratio of alkaline to acid minerals. Raw food follows as a close second, and all our cooked and store-bought processed foods come in at a very distant third.

Is this beginning to make some sense? Great! Let's do a quick review and see that we've answered the two questions that opened this chapter. First, a living food is one that is still growing. Good examples are fruits and vegetables that are eaten within two days of being picked and the still-growing sprouts that you can find in your health food store or supermarket. Using the techniques I share with you in this book, you'll learn how you can easily expand the variety of living food available to you and your family.

Raw food looks very similar to living food except that it is no longer growing. Most living food becomes raw food within twenty-four to forty-eight hours after it has been harvested. (The only exceptions are the sprouts you buy at the store.) Slightly less nutritious, raw food is still very beneficial to our health as long as it is still fresh. Along with living food, it provides an incredible power to heal both the body and the mind.

Finally, there are the cooked or otherwise processed foods that 95 percent of us eat 95 percent of the time. This food has no healing power whatsoever, which is perhaps why many doctors still do not believe that food can heal. There is no way to bring cooked food back to life. Though I do not focus on this type of food in this book, I mention it because the latest nutritional research clearly suggests that this food contributes to many of our illnesses, chronic diseases, and premature deaths. So begin today to substitute living and raw food for cooked food whenever possible.

This book is filled with living and raw food recipes that will increase your energy level and support you in your quest to become healthier. In a relatively short period of time you will find yourself thinking much more clearly and with remarkable focus. Healthwise, you'll find your weight normalizing. Aches and pains you might have suffered with for years will gradually and steadily disappear. Being sick will become a rare event and seldom last for more than a day or two—and you will usually be able to pinpoint what you ate that caused the problem. Perhaps, like me, you may find yourself healing from diseases that have mystified and stymied the medical profession. Living and raw food are amazing rejuvenating agents.

In my food classes I suggest that everyone sets a goal of eating at least 50 percent living and raw food. As impossible as this may sound to you at first, if you make the commitment to prepare at least one new recipe from this book every day, you will eventually reach this goal. You will find that the recipes are delicious, fun and easy to prepare, and most importantly, will make you feel better than ever before.

It may take two weeks, two months, or two years to get to 50 percent, depending on your motivation. Whatever length of time it takes doesn't matter—just do it. When I discovered all this, I knew why I had to start eating mostly living and raw food, and I did it virtually overnight. I am endlessly grateful that I chose to embrace life rather than continue to suffer with disease and rapidly declining health.

In the following chapters we will take a closer look at what science is beginning to discover about living and raw food. Then I will present your road map to better health and give you the vehicle to get you there—the delicious, easy-to-prepare recipes that I was blessed with creating while restoring my own radiant health.

Why Organic?

*O*rganic: Food produced without the use of chemically formulated fertilizers, growth stimulants, antibiotics, or pesticides.

A friend once said to me, "Eating organic is a no-brainer. Would I rather ingest foods laced with chemicals or those that aren't?" She's been a consumer of organic food for over twenty years, and this has been her response whenever the inevitable question Why organic? arises. Seems simple, doesn't it? Yet approximately 90 percent of our vegetables, fruits, grains, and other food is produced with chemical fertilizers, pesticides, and herbicides. Because this information is generally suppressed from the public, most consumers aren't informed enough about the issues to care.

Of course, corporate executives care. Their widely held assumption is that using synthetic chemicals produces greater yields and therefore greater profits. They mistakenly believe that using pesticides means less crop loss from insects and other animal pests and fungus, and that chemical fertilizers increase crop size and volume.

Ironically, recent research tends to contradict this theory. Long-term studies conducted over the past decade indicate comparable yields using organic methods. One grain study showed more profitability of organic farms in harsh weather years, while another study on corn yields found organic farms exceeded conventional farms in years of drought. A five-year research project that studied Midwestern farms concluded that, in dollars per acre, income between organic and conventional farms was the same, although the cost of chemical fertilizer was the equalizing factor. Thus the contention that organic farming is more expensive and therefore less profitable is speculative at best and remains open to debate.

Beyond profit and yield there is a looming price to pay for chemical-based farming in terms of human and environmental health. The cost to our precious Earth includes the pollution of our air and waterways; the depletion of topsoil, arable land, and natural habitat; and the decimation of countless plant and animal species. Dollar for dollar, the equation makes no sense.

Unquestionably, chemical inputs cause extensive damage to our environment; but the inverse is equally astounding. Organic growing methods decrease pesticide contamination, enrich the soil, protect wildlife, safeguard water resources, are economically sound and health supporting, and encourage a self-sustaining ecosystem.

If, as my friend asserts, choosing organic is a no-brainer, then why would anyone knowingly select conventionally grown food? Once people learn the truth (if they have access to it), it usually boils down to a simple matter of cost and availability. Many mainstream supermarkets don't carry organic products, and those that do typically charge significantly more for them. In addition, the prevailing opinion is that conventionally grown food is not harmful and is just as nutritious as organic. This is exactly what the corporate food producers and chemical conglomerates want consumers to believe, and they've done a good job deceiving us.

The media has contributed to this mindset by attempting to discredit organic food. For example, in 2000, a report on an episode of the *20/20* television program incorrectly suggested that organic food could make us sick, due to a new strain of bacteria. The program also erroneously reported that no pesticide residues were present in either organic or conventional produce. The show's host eventually apologized for falsifying evidence and relying on fabricated tests. The motive behind this and other trumped-up stories is not clear, but when misinformation is spread through broad media sources, the harm is deep and far-reaching. These and similar distortions have left the public confused and reluctant to embrace more natural methods of food production.

All food is not created equal. The nutritional content of organically grown produce is superior. It is higher in vitamins, minerals, and naturally occurring enzymes, which make the nutrients in organic food more easily digested and absorbed. Research by Rutgers University indicates that, overall, the nutrients in organic produce are higher by 83 percent, and the concentration of minerals and trace elements is higher by 87 percent. A Tufts University study concluded that organic produce has an 88 percent higher nutrient content. Additionally, organic food contains higher levels of phytochemicals; these are mostly antioxidants that are helpful in countering oxidation caused by free radicals, which are associated with some cancers.

Pesticide residue in and on commercially grown food can alter that food's cellular structure, which may pose a serious problem for those who eat it. Also, there have been several studies linking exposure to pesticides and chemicals to a number of degenerative diseases. The no-brainer component of my friend's argument is that unless we choose organics we will be continually exposed to pesticides through our food, and any related health risks will be unavoidable.

Unfortunately, funding to study the safety and hazards of chemical inputs is terribly inadequate. The little research that has been conducted typically relates to cancer. However, the findings are substantial and irrefutable: agricultural chemicals, including pesticides, are definitively correlated with increases in bladder, kidney, and childhood cancers, and in non-Hodgkin's lymphoma. Additionally, there are reported alterations in DNA, reproductive problems, birth defects, and deleterious effects on the nervous system. The World Health Organization estimates that three million people annually suffer acute pesticide poisoning, primarily in the global agricultural working population. The sad news is that pesticide and herbicide use is on the rise, including those that are known carcinogens.

Among the many rationales for avoiding conventionally grown food is a new and extremely terrifying one: genetically modified organisms (GMOs). GMOs are derived from plants, animals, or microorganisms. Genetic engineering is the transfer of genes from one organism to another through means that do not, and could not, occur in nature. The current corporate trend is to genetically alter many of our staple crops; the top contenders have been corn, soybeans, tomatoes, cotton, and canola (rapeseed). An example of an unsuccessful GMO experiment was the addition of a gene from an Arctic fish into a strawberry to create more frost resistance in the fruit. A popular and highly successful modification has been to incorporate pesticides and other chemicals directly into the genetic makeup of plants to create crops that are more insect resistant and herbicide tolerant. This represents nearly all genetically engineered crops grown today. Of course, whenever these plants are consumed, so are the pesticides contained in their genetic structure.

Organic farmers are extremely concerned about GMOs for multiple reasons. Wind drift can cause crop contamination by both chemicals and pollen. Altered genes, once released into the environment, cannot be recalled.

A molecular biologist funded by the National Institutes of Health stated, "Once a gene is inserted into an organism, it can have unanticipated side effects. Mutations and side effects can cause genetically engineered foods to contain toxins and allergens, and to be reduced in nutritional values." Presently, the Food and Drug Administration does not require labeling of GMO foods or oversee their testing, although consumers and both organic and nonorganic farmers are requesting it. If producers are so certain GMO foods are safe, why not require labeling so consumers can make informed choices? Until then, keep in mind that the next succulent scarlet tomato you enjoy may have an unnatural but cozy bond with a salmon.

Fortunately, the organic movement is gaining strength. At the turn of the millennium, organic farming worldwide had increased tenfold the previous decade. Moreover, retail sales of organics in North America have been growing 20 percent each year.

Those of us who wish to support organics can also contribute locally. If space permits, we can grow our own produce in naturally enriched soil. Organic, homegrown, fresh-picked vegetables and fruits retain their full array of nutrients and life force. The next best alternative is to buy organic produce at local farmers' markets, where most fruits and vegetables are picked that morning or the day before. Usually produce is less expensive at these markets, and supporting local farmers also helps the local economy. Another option is a natural food store. If you don't have one in your area, encourage the produce manager at your supermarket to stock organic fruits and vegetables. This is one small step toward raising the consciousness in your area about organics. As the saying goes: think globally, act locally. And, of course, always choose organics—it's the right choice for you and the planet.

Setting up a Living and Raw Food Kitchen

Setting up a living and raw food kitchen is simple and enjoyable. Much of the equipment you need may already be in your kitchen. If not, you can find it by exploring health food stores, kitchen stores, department stores, mail order catalogs, and online retailers. Some of the equipment may be unfamiliar to you, but none is difficult to operate. Simply follow the manufacturer's instructions and the recipes in this book. Here is a list of items that are useful in a living and raw food kitchen:

Blender, heavy-duty (I recommend the Vita-Mix or K-Tec)

Dehydrator (I recommend Excalibur)

Food processor (I recommend Cuisinart)

Juicer, electric (I prefer Champion)

Bowls (small, medium, and large)

Cake pans

Citrus reamer (small handheld juicer)

Coffee grinder

Colander

Dish rack (for sprouting)

Food chopper (small handheld chopper)

Funnels (small, medium, and large)

Glass pie plates

Glass pitcher

Glass storage containers

Glass storage jars (small, medium, and large)

Grater

Juice bag, nylon stockings, or paint strainer

Knives

Mandolin (manual slicer)

Mason jars (small, medium, and large)

Measuring cups

Measuring spoons

Platters (small, medium, and large)

Rectangular glass pans

Rubber spatulas

Spice jars

Strainer

Thermometer

Vegetable scrub brush

Wire or nylon mesh or cheesecloth

Wooden cutting board

Wooden spoons

Zester

Basics of Soaking and Sprouting

$\mathcal{I}$f you're new to living food, you may not know that you can soak and sprout your own supply of fresh live produce at home. At first you might be inclined to purchase most of your sprouts for convenience. However, I heartily recommend learning how to soak and sprout as much of your food as possible. Not only is it extremely economical, it takes very little time and is surprisingly fun and easy. You can't get fresher than home grown, and you'll have peace of mind knowing that your sprouts contain no pesticides or chemicals. Sprouts are easy to digest and are a rich source of oxygen, enzymes, vitamins, and essential minerals. They are a perfect addition to most of the main dishes, pâtés, salads, and soups that you will be learning to prepare.

Guidelines for Sprouting: Dry Storage

Raw nuts and seeds are an essential staple of the raw living food diet. It is extremely important to always purchase RAW, unroasted nuts and seeds to prepare the recipes in this book. Roasted nuts and seeds are not capable of sprouting because the heat used in the roasting process destroys their ability to germinate. Raw nuts and seeds that are soaked and sprouted become more nutritious and are high in enzymes.

Once nuts or seeds are removed from their protective shells, there is the possibility that the essential oils they contain can become rancid. To prevent this, store raw nuts and seeds in sealed, airtight glass containers in a cool, dry location. Also, you can keep them in the refrigerator for up to a month and in the freezer for up to six months.

It's not crucial to store beans and whole grains in the refrigerator, but keeping them cool and dry will extend their shelf life.

Soaking: Seeds, Grains, and Dried Beans

All raw seeds, grains, and dried beans are brought to life when placed in water. Unless otherwise specified, purified room temperature water is best. You can do the soaking wherever you have the space and where the ambient temperature is moderate (neither too hot nor too cold). Small seeds (such as alfalfa and clover) and small grains (such as quinoa) should be soaked for about 5 hours. Hulled seeds (such as sunflower and pumpkin) will become soft after 6 to 8 hours of soaking. Large grains (such as wheat and rye) and large beans (such as mung, garbanzos, and lentils) will be ready to germinate in about 12 hours.

Soaking can be done in any nonmetallic container. I like to use glass jars so I can watch the sprouts grow. I cover the jars with a piece of nylon screen or cotton cheesecloth held in place by a rubber band. This makes rinsing them very easy. Soaked seeds, grains, and beans should be drained and rinsed every 6 to 8 hours and fresh water added.

Germination

After soaking, the seeds, grains, and beans should be drained, rinsed well, and put back in their containers. At this stage they need to be kept moist but not wet, and they should have access to air, which the nylon screen or cheesecloth allows. They also need to be kept in the dark (which simulates being planted in soil) and at a comfortable room temperature. Good places to consider for the germination phase are a closet, under a towel, or in a covered box. During this period it's important to rinse your "babies" twice a day. I usually do this in the morning when I awaken and in the evening before I retire. This way they are regularly cleaned and refreshed.

Everything in your sprout garden, except the very small seeds (such as alfalfa, clover, radish, and cabbage), will be ready to harvest when the sprout is as long as its founding seed. This usually happens within 1 to 4 days. These mature sprouts should be rinsed and drained thoroughly one last time before they join the soaked nuts in your refrigerator.

Greening

The final stage for the small seeds begins when two little leaves emerge. At this time the sprouts should be placed in indirect light to activate the greening process, which will produce the chlorophyll that is so healing to us. Caring for sprouts at this juncture is the same as during germination: rinse and drain well every 12 hours.

After 1 or 2 days the leaves on these sprouts will turn green; the sprouts are then ready to be harvested. You should gently swish the sprouts in a basin of water to loosen and remove the seed hulls. This will keep the sprouts fresher for a longer period of time. After you've rinsed the sprouts, be sure to drain them well before putting them in the refrigerator for storage. Most sprouts will keep for at least 1 week in the refrigerator, especially if they are rinsed and drained well every 3 days.

How to Use Living Food

Soaked nuts and seeds and sprouted seeds and grains are vibrant living foods that have many practical uses. Soaked nuts and sunflower and pumpkin seeds are wonderful to use in making delicious milks, pâtés, salad dressings, dehydrated snacks, and pie crusts. Sprouted grains are great in milks and dehydrated breads and crackers, or for use as a cereal. Sprouted beans add high-quality nutrition and a distinctive quality to salads and casseroles. Green sprouts from the small seeds have a potent life force and make excellent salad toppers. They can also be used in raw vegetable juices.

The more that you experiment with these amazing living foods, the more you will appreciate their vital energies. Enjoy the countless delights they provide.

Soaking and Sprouting Step by Step

Step 1   Measure the seeds, nuts, grains, or legumes. Put them into a fine-mesh colander and rinse. Transfer to a glass jar and cover with pure water to reach 3 or 4 inches above the seeds. Let the seeds soak overnight or for the specified amount of time. The water awakens the plant enzymes within the seeds, triggering the life force that initiates the sprouting cycle.

Step 2   Place a wire mesh screen on the top of the glass jar to prevent the seeds from washing away. Drain the soak water (and hulls); this will discard the enzyme inhibitors. Rinse the seeds with pure water; then drain again.

Step 3   Let the seeds rest in the glass jar on the kitchen counter (or another dark place) for 12 to 24 hours. Keep the jar tilted at a 45-degree angle for the best drainage. Rinse and drain twice a day until the desired sprout tails appear.

Step 4   Expose the sprouts to indirect sunlight for about 6 hours to green them and activate their abundance of chlorophyll. Enjoy!

Introduction

Growing Sunflower, Wheatgrass, and Buckwheat Sprouts

Step 1 Soak the seeds or grains for 6 to 8 hours (preferably at bedtime). Do not soak longer than 8 hours, as the seeds and grains will mold. Use the following amounts as a guideline:

> 3 cups unhulled striped sunflower seeds
> 2 cups black sunflower seeds
> 1½ cups hard winter wheat berries
> 1½ cups unhulled buckwheat groats

Step 2 Drain the water in the morning (or after 6 to 8 hours) and rinse.

Step 3 Let drain for 20 to 24 hours, or until a sprouted tip emerges from the end of the seed or grain. Rinse every 12 hours. Drain at a 45-degree angle.

Step 4 Put 1 inch of organic potting soil in a starter seed tray. Fortify the soil with a level tablespoon of powdered kelp, or add liquid kelp to your watering can (follow the directions on the label for mixing). Water until moist but not drenched.

Step 5 Spread the seeds or grains in a single layer so they are just touching. Cover with another starter seed tray and add some weight to the tray (filled jugs of water, heavy stones, or thick books are just a few possible items that could be used as weights). If you are preparing several trays, stack them and add some weight to the top tray. Otherwise, add about 2 pounds of weight to the tray. This will help to hold down the tray and put pressure on the seeds.

Step 6 Put the tray in a room with an ambient temperature of at least 55 degrees or above. Do not put the tray in direct sunlight, as it will be too hot for the seeds. Let the seeds rest for at least 3 days; do not water them.

Step 7 Uncover the trays when the sprouts are about 1 inch tall. Place them in the sunlight and water them once a day, just until moist, for 4 days or until the sprouts are at least 6 inches tall.

Step 8 Harvest the greens as needed or store them in the refrigerator.

Sprouting Chart

Plant Variety	Method of Sprouting	Amount per Quart Jar	Soaking Time (hours)	Rinses per Day
Adzuki beans	jar	½ cup	12	2
Alfalfa seeds	jar or tray	2 tbsp.	6	2
Buckwheat groats	jar	1 cup	8–14	2
Cabbage seeds	jar	3 tbsp.	4–6	2
Chinese cabbage seeds	jar	3 tbsp.	12	2
Clover seeds	jar or tray	2 tbsp.	6	2
Corn	jar	1½ cups	10–14	2
Fenugreek	jar or soil	¼ cup	8	2
Flaxseeds*	bowl	—	4–6	—
Garbanzo beans (chickpeas)	jar	1 cup	12	2
Lentils	jar	¾ cup	8–12	2
Lettuce seeds	jar or soil	3 tbsp.	6	2
Mung beans	jar	½ cup	12	2
Mustard seeds	jar or soil	3 tbsp.	6	2
Oat groats	jar	1½ cups	8–12	2
Peanuts	jar	1 cup	8	2
Peas	jar or soil	2 cups	8	2
Pumpkin seeds	jar	1½ cups	8	2
Quinoa	jar	⅓ cup	4–8	2
Radish seeds	jar or soil	3 tbsp.	4–8	2
Rye berries	jar or soil	1 cup	12	2
Sesame seeds	jar	2 cups	4–6	2
Soybeans	jar	¾ cup	8	2
Wheat berries (hard)	jar or soil	1 cup	8	2
Wheat berries (soft)	jar or soil	1 cup	8	2

* Flaxseeds are sprouted by soaking in a bowl for 4 to 6 hours. Do not rinse.

Introduction

Food Dehydration

Dehydrating is an age-old method of food preservation. It involves the simple drying of food by removing water through evaporation. The traditional technique for dehydrating food uses the sun to draw out and evaporate moisture. A more modern version uses electric dehydrating equipment, many of which allow for greater control over the temperature.

Dehydrated food retains most of its nutrients and vital life force. An ancient tomb recently excavated in Egypt revealed some very old dehydrated grains. Surprisingly, when the grains were soaked, they sprouted. In the *Essene Gospel of Peace* by Edmond Bordeaux Székely there is a reference to food dehydration in the form of bread-making. The Essenes would soak wheat until it sprouted, crush it, and place it in the sun to dry. Perhaps their results were the prototype for our present-day bread!

Used since the dawn of civilization, food dehydration has withstood the test of time. Primitive people sun dried a variety of food, such as berries, roots, and meats. Later, fishing cultures laid their catches out to dry. Additionally, fisherman and voyagers used dried food for sustenance on long journeys, which helped to prevent diseases like beriberi and scurvy. Native Americans relied on sun-dried fruits, meats, and even corn. Perhaps the Pilgrims were actually giving thanks for learning this skill from the Indians, one which aided the European settlers through many long winters.

More recent societies also dehydrated food. The pioneers of the West endured long journeys and harsh conditions by maintaining their strength through eating dried fruits and vegetables. In the early twentieth century, before the luxury of modern refrigeration, many families relied on food preservation by drying. During the World Wars, provisions were significantly augmented by dehydrated food. Rationing during World War II necessitated the dehydration of food to preserve every single morsel. The federal government even developed and offered plans for people to construct their own solar dehydrators. Today the military still embraces the use of dehydrated food because of its ease of transport, long shelf life, and intrinsic nutritional value. Clearly, this historic reference is strong testimony to the benefit of dehydrated food as a sustainer of life.

Even though with the coming of the refrigeration age dehydration was used less frequently as a way to preserve food, many people striving for a healthier lifestyle are rediscovering its numerous advantages. It is compact, versatile, easy to transport, convenient, nutritious, and tastes great. It can be eaten as a snack, served as an accompaniment to other foods, or used as an ingredient in recipes. Are you a camper, hiker, or traveler? Dehydrated food is the ideal choice, as it is lightweight and easily portable.

Dehydrated living food, such as nuts, seeds, and crackers, keeps variety in the diet with an array of tastes and textures, while adding a pleasing crunch. When properly prepared, dehydrated food can even replicate the taste and texture of cooked food. Eating dehydrated food eases the transition from a diet of cooked food to one based on raw and living food. Dehydrating can also enhance a food's enticing flavor and appealing texture and color.

Dehydrators allow us to enjoy warm food without destroying its life-giving enzymes and nutrients, an important factor for those of us who crave warm food during colder months. Using a dehydrator offers countless creative cuisine options and can help us design raw food menus that are varied and stimulating. Many main dishes prepared and warmed in a dehydrator, such as raw vegetable spaghetti and ravioli ("raw-violis") and soups, can add warmth and interest to your dinner preparations. They are especially comforting for wintertime meals. Also, the dehydrator itself can be utilized as a food warmer, to gently reheat foods if desired.

Electric dehydrators that are efficient and economical are readily available through health food stores, department stores, mail order catalogs, and retail sites on the Web. These operate using fans and heating elements that allow you to regulate the temperature. To retain its life force, active enzymes, and vitamins, food should be dehydrated at 120 degrees or lower. I highly recommend Excalibur as the brand of choice, as it has removable trays that easily adjust for foods of various heights. Also, the fan and heating element are in the back. This evenly disperses the heat so the trays don't need to be rotated, as they must with other brands. I've found the Excalibur to be extremely dependable. In fact, I've had mine for nine years; I use it weekly and have never had a problem with it.

Once your food is dehydrated, it should be stored in tightly covered glass jars. Because foods that are completely dry have an extended shelf life, seeds, chips, and crackers and dehydrated fruit and soaked dehydrated nuts can be stored for six months or longer. A few years ago I had prepared a batch of crackers. I stored them in a glass jar under a sink cabinet and totally forgot about them. Much to my amazement, when I discovered them six months later they were still crispy and delicious. I had no idea they could remain pristine that long! Most dehydrated food will not keep as long as my crackers in the cabinet. Softer dehydrated foods, such as breads, cookies, and some main dishes, require a greater amount of moisture, so they should only be stored for one week.

Moisture in the air can cause some foods to rehydrate; if this happens, dry the food in the dehydrator for a short time. If a food is dehydrated too long and becomes hard and dry, simply dunk it in water or mist the surface lightly.

Maintaining a Raw Food Diet

*W*hen people first embark on the raw food adventure, they often feel like a solo traveler or someone from another planet. Eating a diet similar to the rest of society provides a common bond. Even our families may treat us like foreigners unless they're sharing our raw food meals. When the rest of our family is still eating cooked food, we can also be challenged by the addictive qualities of these foods. Because heat releases flavors and aromas and breaks down the fiber in food (making it easier to chew and eat large amounts), cooked food can be tantalizing.

It's no wonder that we can feel isolated. Perhaps the most important factor in sticking to our commitment to healthy living is to locate kindred spirits for support. One way to find like-minded people and get emotional support is to participate in a raw food potluck. If there isn't one in your area, start one of your own. Potlucks offer a great opportunity to network, learn from others, share recipes, and keep ourselves on track. If there isn't a raw food restaurant near you, potlucks can provide a chance for you to socialize while having a superb meal away from home. At the same time, you can share information and resources (such as sources for bulk foods) and exchange recipes. Often people set out a copy of their recipe alongside their dish, so you get to taste it and take the list of ingredients home with you! Before long, you'll have a collection of recipes for new favorite foods to provide you with inspiration and support.

If you are unable to find like-minded friends near you, online discussion boards provide another option to connect with people who are also following a raw food lifestyle. You can share opinions and ideas and find out about upcoming conferences and events. Web sites offer an abundance of information, too. Three of my favorite sites are:

www.rawfood.com
www.living-foods.com
www.rawtimes.com

Conferences give us yet another opportunity to get together, and sometimes we can even meet our online friends in person. These types of gatherings usually include presentations by raw food authors and experts. We can see food and equipment demonstrations, try new recipes, and eat beautiful, delicious meals prepared by raw food chefs, authors, and caterers.

Dehydrated food will help you ease into a raw diet, because many dehydrated foods reflect the flavors and textures of cooked food. Once your new lifestyle is firmly established, dehydrated food will keep your diet interesting and exciting. Also, having dehydrated food always on hand will provide you with quick, healthful, satisfying snacks when hunger strikes.

To keep your meals interesting, prepare imaginative, eye-appealing dishes with complex flavors. While it's helpful to have a few favorites to rotate among, your diet will hold greater interest if you commit to trying at least one or two new recipes each week. One of the many wonderful aspects of raw food recipes is that they are so easy to adapt according to our own preferences. Feel free to experiment to achieve the flavors and consistencies you most prefer or remind you of cooked food favorites. It's easy to do, and it's fun!

Once you have adopted your new lifestyle, set aside time to hear talks or attend classes conducted by experts. Read books and articles to stay on top of the latest information and research. Two wonderful books are *Conscious Eating* by Gabriel Cousens, MD, and *The Sun Food Diet Success System* by David Wolfe. For more selections, see the Recommended Reading section (page 308).

An important key to success is always using the freshest, most flavorful ingredients. Shop at farmers' markets where you can get high-quality organic food for very reasonable prices. Get acquainted with the farmers—they're a valuable resource to us and our communities. Organic farmers, in particular, are making an important contribution to the future of our health and environment, and your support of their efforts will encourage the increase of organic foods in general.

Allot time every day for deep breathing and sitting in stillness. Meditation and mindful awareness are important tools to our success and contentment with a raw food lifestyle. The more we observe our body and "inner voice," the better attuned we will be to our needs and the more we will understand how to meet them.

As your body heals and rejuvenates, you may discover that you need more rest. Initially you may experience a "healing crisis" as your body releases toxins and your system readjusts. Trust your body's internal wisdom and honor its request for additional downtime; sleep and rest when your body wants it.

Finally, spread the word about your new lifestyle. Talking to people presents opportunities for networking and support. You may be surprised at the number of people who are sincerely interested, and by sharing what you know you will be planting seeds that inspire others along this incredible path of health and rejuvenation.

Young Coconuts

Coconuts are one of the healthiest foods we can eat. In their early stages of growth, between six and nine months, coconuts are at their peak of tenderness and nutrition. These young coconuts contain more water than older coconuts, and their pulp is the softest, sweetest, and most flavorful. This makes them superior for both our health and use in recipes. At sea, coconuts can literally be a life-saving treasure, since coconuts can float and they contain sterile water.

The medicinal properties of coconuts are legendary. Coconuts are rich in lauric acid, a fatty acid with antibacterial, antiviral, antifungal, and anti-inflammatory qualities. The body converts lauric acid to monolaurin, which nutritional research has indicated may deactivate a variety of pathogens including several viruses (influenza, herpes simplex, measles, and pneumonia), several bacteria, and HIV.

Coconut oil has been shown in a few small studies to reduce the viral load in patients with HIV infection, helping them to gain weight and prolonging their lives. It's thought that HIV viruses take in fat molecules from coconut oil, but these molecules disintegrate the viruses' outer coatings. Although much work remains to be done to show that coconut oil can have a positive effect in large numbers of people, it's exciting to think that it could provide an economical and accessible remedy for this terrible disease.

Coconut water is nearly identical to human blood plasma and is known to have been used in emergency transfusions when there is a lack of standard intravenous fluid. Researchers report that coconut water is high in potassium, copper, iron, and calcium. Coconut water is also high in ascorbic acid (vitamin C) and the B-complex vitamins, and it is a rich source of electrolytes, with the electrolytic balance being the same as in human blood.

Crack open a coconut and discover even more health-promoting attributes. The pulp and oil are reputed to lower cholesterol; improve the symptoms of Crohn's disease and other digestive disorders; reduce the risk of heart disease; aid in the treatment of diabetes and chronic fatigue; and promote healthy metabolic functioning. The oil is invaluable for combating fungal infections, skin rashes, and plantar warts. It can also be used as a wrinkle preventative and skin rejuvenator.

Aside from the health benefits, the young coconut's pulp and water are simply delightful and delicious. The water can be used as a nutritious beverage or recipe ingredient. Its pulp and water can help reduce a desire for sweets because their delicate sweet taste satisfies naturally. Coconuts are also very low in sugar. Once you taste them, you'll agree that they are indeed all they're cracked up to be! If you cannot find an Asian market in your area that sells young coconuts, check for retailers on the Web.

I was first introduced to the value of young coconuts at Dr. Gabriel Cousens' Tree of Life Rejuvenation Center in Patagonia, Arizona. I found that by using young coconuts I could create even more diverse and ingenious recipes, particularly desserts. It is extremely rewarding to prepare desserts that are so delicious people find it difficult to believe that they're completely raw.

Coconut pulp is extremely versatile and very useful for achieving the proper texture and flavor for pies, puddings, and parfaits. It has the perfect consistency and mild taste for smoothies and soups. The pulp also makes a luscious pasta replacement. Just cut it into julienne strips and warm it in the dehydrator; the result will be the texture and taste of a noodle.

I love coconut water "straight" as a nutritious drink, or combined with scrumptious nut milks to add sweetness and flavor. Blend coconut water with soaked nuts and then strain it through layers of cheesecloth or any of the products available for straining juices or nut milks. The resulting milk is delicious as a beverage or a recipe ingredient, and it is luxurious in soups.

A few years ago, I was asked to participate at the Raw Food Culinary Showcase in Jamaica. This was a gathering of raw food chefs and lecturers from around the world. At the resort was an outdoor snack bar, where coconuts were readily available for eating and drinking. I later learned that more coconuts were consumed in one day than in any other day in the entire history of the snack bar. This sure gives new meaning to the term health (coco)nuts!

Helpful Hints

Food

1. Always buy fresh organic food at its peak of ripeness. The recipes will only be as good as the food that goes into them.

2. Purchase organic bottled spices or loose spices from the bulk food section of your health food store. Store bulk spices in glass jars, and buy small quantities so the spices will always be fresh. Conventional grocery stores sell spices that have been irradiated.

3. Shop at farmers' markets for fresh organic food at great prices. Support organic farmers!

4. Hemp seeds are a perfectly balanced food with all the essential fatty acids. Add them to recipes or sprinkle them over your food as a nutritious topping.

5. Grow your own green sprouts and eat some every day.

6. Use a high-quality sea salt. I prefer Celtic salt or RealSalt (brand name) in all my food preparation. My favorite is RealSalt because of its sweet flavor and fine consistency. Look for it in your health food store or check the Resource Guide (page 308) for mail order sources.

7. Always buy high-quality oils that are packaged in dark glass or black plastic containers, as these will protect the oils from exposure to light, which can destroy their delicate properties. There are a number of recommended brands mentioned in the Resource Guide (page 308).

8. Wash your fruits and vegetables when you bring them home from the store or farmers' market. This way you can quickly and easily prepare a dish when hunger strikes.

9. Use raw carob powder as a substitute for cocoa powder.

Equipment

1. Replace the blades for your food processor or have them sharpened on a regular basis.

2. Buy a good set of knives and sharpen them weekly.

3. Purchase a high-speed blender as soon as your budget allows. I recommend a Vita-Mix or K-Tec.

4. Store food in glass containers.

5. Save cake pans, molds, bundt pans, or pie plates, and use them to mold raw cakes, pies, and other desserts.

6. Flea markets and garage sales are great places to find a used dehydrator or juicer. Make sure the dehydrator has a thermostat.

Food Preparation

1. If the amount of food in a recipe is too large to be processed effectively in your equipment, process one-half or one-third of the recipe at a time, and then combine the portions after processing.

2. Soak nuts and seeds in a cool place, and be sure to rinse them at least twice a day. Soaked nuts and seeds are easier to digest.

3. For recipes, always measure nuts and seeds prior to soaking them.

4. For recipes, always measure flaxseeds prior to grinding them.

5. If a Champion Juicer or a Green Power Juicer is not available to make nut pâtés, a food processor fitted with the S blade may be used instead. When using a food processor, be sure to add $\frac{1}{4}$ to $\frac{1}{2}$ cup of water with the nuts or seeds to make the pâté smooth and creamy.

6. If your dehydrated food becomes too moist, put it back in the dehydrator for about 2 hours. Always store dehydrated food in an airtight glass container.

7. Crackers can be made out of leftover raw soup. Just add some soaked flaxseeds and dehydrate.

Blanching Almonds

Blanching removes the brown skin of shelled almonds. It's easy and quick to do, and blanching enhances the color and flavor of many dishes. Soak almonds for 12 to 48 hours. Drain and transfer them to a heatproof bowl. Pour boiling water over the almonds to cover them completely. Let them rest for 30 to 60 seconds, just until the skins are loosened. Drain the boiling water and add some warm water. This helps to keep the almonds moist and will facilitate the removal of the skin. Peel the almonds by squeezing them between your index or middle finger and thumb. The skins should slide off easily.

Breakfast

Almond Blueberry Porridge

yield: 2 servings

1 cup	almonds, soaked 12–48 hours
1 cup	coconut water
2 cups	young coconut pulp
1 cup	fresh blueberries
1 teaspoon	vanilla extract

Combine the almonds and coconut water in a blender or a food processor fitted with the S blade and process until smooth and creamy. Add the coconut pulp, ¾ cup of the blueberries, and the vanilla and process until smooth. Serve with the remaining blueberries as a garnish.

Almond Peach Breakfast Smoothie

yield: 2 servings

1½ cups	coconut water
1 cup	young coconut pulp
1	apple
1	ripe peach
½ cup	almonds, soaked 12–48 hours

Combine all the ingredients in a blender and process until smooth and creamy.

Almond Pumpkin Seed Granola

yield: 1 serving

¹⁄₂ cup	almonds, soaked 12–48 hours
2 tablespoons	pumpkins seeds, soaked 6–8 hours
2 tablespoons	sunflower seeds, soaked 4–6 hours
¹⁄₂	apple, grated
¹⁄₄ cup	young coconut water, water, or nut milk
¹⁄₄ cup	fresh blueberries (optional)
2 tablespoons	golden flaxseeds, ground
1 tablespoon	raisins
Pinch	ground cinnamon

Combine the almonds, pumpkin seeds, and sunflower seeds in a food processor fitted with the S blade and process into a fine meal. Transfer to a small bowl and stir in the apple, coconut water, optional blueberries, flaxseeds, raisins, and cinnamon.

Autumn Porridge

yield: 3–4 servings

2 cups	peeled, seeded, and chopped butternut squash
1 cup	walnuts, soaked 1 hour
1 cup	coconut water or water
1 tablespoon	orange zest
2 teaspoons	ground cinnamon
2 teaspoons	vanilla extract

Combine ½ cup of the butternut squash, ¾ cup of the walnuts, the coconut water, orange zest, cinnamon, and vanilla in a blender and process until smooth and creamy. Combine the remaining walnuts and squash in a food processor fitted with the S blade and process until finely chopped. Add to the blended mixture and stir until well combined.

Cashew Apple Porridge

yield: 3–4 servings

2 cups	cashews, soaked 1 hour
1–2 cups	young coconut water
2	apples (1 chopped, 1 diced)
1 cup	young coconut pulp
2 teaspoons	vanilla extract
1½ teaspoons	ground cinnamon

Combine the cashews, coconut water, chopped apple, coconut pulp, vanilla, and cinnamon in a blender. Process until smooth and creamy. Stir in the diced apple and garnish with a sprinkle of cinnamon.

Buckwheat Cereal

yield: 4–8 servings

2–4 cups	buckwheat
Pinch	ground cinnamon (optional)

Soak the buckwheat for 8–12 hours. Sprout for approximately two days, rinsing at least three times a day. (Rinsing is extremely important; otherwise the buckwheat will ferment.) Sprinkle with the cinnamon, if using. Place on a dehydrator tray and dehydrate for 6–8 hours at 105 degrees or until dry and crispy.

Cranberry Porridge

yield: 2 servings

1½ cups	young coconut pulp
¼–½ cup	coconut water
¼ cup	pitted dates (optional)
1 teaspoon	vanilla extract
½ cup	hazelnuts, soaked 4–6 hours
¼ cup	fresh cranberries

Combine ¾ cup of the coconut pulp, the coconut water, dates, and vanilla in a blender and process until smooth and creamy. Combine the hazelnuts, the remaining ¾ cup coconut pulp, and the cranberries in a food processor fitted with the S blade and pulse or process until coarsely chopped. Add to the blended mixture and stir until well combined.

Breakfast

Divine Orange Porridge

yield: 2 servings

³/₄–1 cup	coconut water
¹/₄ cup	macadamia nuts, soaked 1 hour
2 cups	young coconut pulp
¹/₄ cup	peeled, seeded, and chopped butternut squash
1 tablespoon	orange zest
2 teaspoons	vanilla extract
	Stevia for desired sweetness,
	or ¹/₄ cup pitted dates (optional)

Combine the coconut water and macadamia nuts in a blender and process briefly. Add the coconut pulp, squash, orange zest, vanilla, and stevia and process until smooth and creamy.

Granola

This granola will keep for one to three months, so make a lot!

2 cups	almonds, soaked 12–48 hours
1 cup	pumpkin seeds, soaked 8 hours
1 cup	sunflower seeds, soaked 4–6 hours
2	apples
1 tablespoon	ground cinnamon
1 teaspoon	Celtic salt
½ cup	raisins (optional)

Place the almonds in a food processor fitted with the S blade and pulse or process until chopped and chunky. Transfer to a bowl. Place the pumpkin seeds and sunflower seeds in a food processor and pulse or process until chopped and chunky. Combine with the almonds. Chop the apples into large pieces and shred them in a food processor. Add to the nuts along with the cinnamon and salt and mix well.

Spread the mixture on a dehydrator tray with a Teflex sheet, and dehydrate for 20–24 hours at 105 degrees or until the desired crispness is achieved. Be sure to dehydrate until all the moisture is removed from the granola. Stir in the raisins, if using. Store the granola in a glass jar. Serve with your favorite nut milk.

Pecan Porridge

yield: 2–3 servings

2 cups	young coconut pulp
1 cup	pecans, soaked 1 hour
2 teaspoons	ground cinnamon
1 teaspoon	vanilla extract
	Coconut water or water as needed
1 tablespoon	golden flaxseeds, ground

Combine the coconut pulp, pecans, cinnamon, and vanilla in a blender and process until smooth and creamy. Add a little coconut water as needed to achieve the desired consistency. Sprinkle each serving with some of the ground flaxseeds. Serve with your favorite nut milk.

Beverages

Nut Milks

A high-quality, high-speed blender works best for making nut milks and is worth the investment. I use a Vita-Mix; another excellent choice is the K-Tec Champ. Nut milk bags can be purchased at www.purejoylivingfoods.com. A paint strainer available at paint stores also works well.

Almond Milk

yield: 1 quart

2 cups	water
1 cup	almonds, soaked 12–48 hours
2 cups	young coconut water
2 teaspoons	vanilla extract

Combine the water and almonds in a blender and process until smooth. Strain through a piece of cheesecloth, a nut milk bag, or a nylon stocking. Stir in the coconut water and vanilla. Store in a glass container in the refrigerator.

Almond Cashew Milk

yield: 1 quart

2 cups	water
1/2 cup	almonds, soaked 12–48 hours
1/2 cup	cashews, soaked 4 hours
2 cups	young coconut water
2 teaspoons	vanilla extract

Combine the water, almonds, and cashews in a blender and process until smooth. Strain through a piece of cheesecloth, a nut milk bag, or a nylon stocking. Stir in the coconut water and vanilla. Store in a glass container in the refrigerator.

Beverages

Almond Sesame Milk

yield: 1 quart

2 cups	water
1/2 cup	almonds, soaked 12–48 hours
1/2 cup	sesame seeds, soaked 6–8 hours
2 cups	young coconut water
2 teaspoons	vanilla extract

Combine the water, almonds, and sesame seeds in a blender and process until smooth. Strain through a piece of cheesecloth, a nut milk bag, or a nylon stocking. Stir in the coconut water and vanilla. Store in a glass container in the refrigerator.

Carob Milk

yield: 1 quart

This makes a great replacement for hot chocolate.

2 cups	water
1 cup	almonds, soaked 12–48 hours
2 cups	young coconut water
2–4 tablespoons	raw carob powder
2 teaspoons	vanilla extract

Combine the water and almonds in a blender and process until smooth. Strain through a piece of cheesecloth, a nut milk bag, or a nylon stocking. Stir in the coconut water, carob powder, and vanilla. Serve warm. Store leftovers in a glass container in the refrigerator.

Beverages

Cashew Nut Milk

yield: 1 quart

2 cups	water
1 cup	cashews, soaked 4 hours
2 cups	young coconut water
2 teaspoons	vanilla extract

Combine the water and cashews in a blender and process until smooth. Strain through a piece of cheesecloth, a nut milk bag, or a nylon stocking. Stir in the coconut water and vanilla. Store in a glass container in the refrigerator.

Chai

Chai is made with equal parts tea and almond milk. My favorite tea is Bengal Spice. You can also purchase a tea called chai, which is typically spiced with cardamom, cinnamon, cloves, ginger, nutmeg, and pepper. I recommend the decaffeinated teas.

Tea
Almond milk
Stevia or honey

Make tea as usual. As the tea steeps, lightly warm an equal amount of almond milk over very low heat. Combine the tea with the warm milk. Sweeten with stevia or honey to taste.

Chai Nut Milk

yield: 1 quart

2 cups	water
1 cup	almonds, soaked 12–48 hours
2 cups	young coconut water
2 teaspoons	vanilla extract
1 teaspoon	garam masala
1 teaspoon	ground ginger
1 teaspoon	ground cinnamon
½ teaspoon	ground cardamom
	Stevia powder

Combine the water and almonds in a blender and process until smooth. Strain through a piece of cheesecloth, a nut milk bag, or a nylon stocking. Stir in the coconut water, vanilla, garam masala, ginger, cinnamon, and cardamom. Sweeten with stevia powder to taste. Store in a glass container in the refrigerator.

Beverages

Chai Smoothie

yield: 1 quart

2 cups	young coconut pulp
1–2 cups	young coconut water
1	frozen banana
1–3 teaspoons	raw carob powder
1 teaspoon	grated fresh ginger
1 teaspoon	vanilla extract
½ teaspoon	ground cinnamon
⅛ teaspoon	ground nutmeg

Combine all the ingredients in a blender and process until smooth and creamy. Add additional coconut water as needed to achieve the desired consistency.

Hazelnut Milk

yield: 1 quart

2 cups	water
1 cup	hazelnuts, soaked 8 hours
2 cups	young coconut water
1 teaspoon	ground cinnamon
¼ teaspoon	ground nutmeg

Combine the water and hazelnuts in a blender and process until smooth. Strain through a piece of cheesecloth, a nut milk bag, or a nylon stocking. Stir in the coconut water, cinnamon, and nutmeg. Store in a glass container in the refrigerator.

Nut Nog

yield: 1 quart

2 cups	water
1 cup	almonds, soaked 6–8 hours
2 cups	young coconut water
2 teaspoons	vanilla extract
1 teaspoon	ground nutmeg
1/2 teaspoon	ground cinnamon
	Stevia or blended dates

Combine the water and almonds in a blender and process until smooth. Strain through a piece of cheesecloth, a nut milk bag, or a nylon stocking. Stir in the coconut water, vanilla, nutmeg, and cinnamon. Sweeten with stevia or blended dates to taste. Store in a glass container in the refrigerator.

Pecan Nut Milk

yield: 1 quart

2 cups	water
1 cup	pecans, soaked 1 hour
2 cups	young coconut water
2 teaspoons	vanilla extract

Combine the water and pecans in a blender and process until smooth. Strain through a piece of cheesecloth, a nut milk bag, or a nylon stocking. Stir in the coconut water and vanilla. Store in a glass container in the refrigerator.

Pecan Carob Nut Milk

yield: 1 quart

2 cups	water
1 cup	pecans, soaked 1 hour
2 cups	young coconut water
1 tablespoon	raw carob powder
2 teaspoons	vanilla extract

Combine the water and pecans in a blender and process until smooth. Strain through a piece of cheesecloth, a nut milk bag, or a nylon stocking. Stir in the coconut water, carob powder, and vanilla. Store in a glass container in the refrigerator.

Beverages

Sesame Milk

yield: 1 quart

2 cups	water
½ cup	hulled white sesame seeds
2 cups	young coconut water
2 teaspoons	vanilla extract

Combine the water and sesame seeds in a blender and process until smooth. Strain through a piece of cheesecloth, a nut milk bag, or a nylon stocking. Stir in the coconut water and vanilla. Store in a glass container in the refrigerator.

Strawberry Milk

yield: 1 quart

Children of all ages will love this drink!

2 cups	water
1 cup	almonds, soaked 12–48 hours
1 cup	fresh strawberries
2 cups	young coconut water
2 teaspoons	vanilla extract

Combine the water, almonds, and strawberries in a blender and process until smooth. Strain through a piece of cheesecloth, a nut milk bag, or a nylon stocking. Stir in the coconut water and vanilla. Store in a glass container in the refrigerator.

Beverages

Walnut Milk

yield: 1 quart

2 cups	water
1 cup	walnuts, soaked 8 hours
2 cups	young coconut water
2 teaspoons	vanilla extract

Combine the water and walnuts in a blender and process until smooth. Strain through a piece of cheesecloth, a nut milk bag, or a nylon stocking. Stir in the coconut water and vanilla. Store in a glass container in the refrigerator.

Smoothies

Apple Banana Smoothie

yield: 1–2 servings

1 cup	young coconut pulp
1 cup	young coconut water or water
1	apple
1	ripe banana
1 teaspoon	vanilla extract

Combine all the ingredients in a blender and process until smooth.

Beverages

Berry Surprise

yield: 1–2 servings

1 cup	frozen berries (any kind)
1 cup	young coconut pulp
1 cup	young coconut water or water
2 tablespoons	raw cashew butter
1 teaspoon	vanilla extract

Combine all the ingredients in a blender and process until smooth.

Blueberry Kiss

yield: 1–2 servings

1 cup	fresh or frozen blueberries
1	frozen banana
1/2–1 cup	young coconut water or water

Combine all the ingredients in a blender and process until smooth.

Carob Banana Smoothie

yield: 1–2 servings

1	frozen banana
1 cup	young coconut pulp
1/2–1 cup	young coconut water or water
2 tablespoons	raw carob powder

Combine all the ingredients in a blender and process until smooth.

Heavenly Fruit Smoothie

yield: 1–2 servings

1	frozen banana
1	ripe peach
1 cup	frozen mango
1/2–1 cup	young coconut water or water
1/4 cup	fresh or frozen blueberries

Combine all the ingredients in a blender and process until smooth.

Peach Smoothie

yield: 1–2 servings

2	ripe peaches
1	frozen banana
½ cup	young coconut water or water

Combine all the ingredients in a blender and process until smooth.

Mango Banana Smoothie

yield: 1–2 servings

1 large	ripe mango, cut into chunks
1	frozen banana
½	apple
1 cup	young coconut water or water
½ cup	young coconut pulp
2 teaspoons	vanilla extract
Pinch	ground cardamom

Combine all the ingredients in a blender and process until smooth.

Kiwi Cooler

yield: 1–2 servings

1	frozen banana
1	kiwifruit, peeled
½ cup	fresh or frozen strawberries
½–1 cup	young coconut water or water

Combine all the ingredients in a blender and process until smooth.

Pear Coconut Smoothie

yield: 1–2 servings

1 cup	young coconut pulp
1 cup	young coconut water or water
1	ripe pear
1	apple
½	frozen banana
2 teaspoons	vanilla extract

Combine all the ingredients in a blender and process until smooth.

Piña Colada Smoothie

yield: 1–2 servings

1 cup	young coconut pulp
1 cup	frozen pineapple
¹/₂–1 cup	young coconut water or water

Combine all the ingredients in a blender and process until smooth.

Pineapple Orange Mixer

yield: 1–2 servings

1 cup	frozen pineapple
1	frozen banana
1	orange
¹/₄–¹/₂ cup	young coconut water or water
¹/₄ cup	fresh orange juice
1 teaspoon	vanilla extract

Combine all the ingredients in a blender and process until smooth.

Raspberry Cooler

yield: 1–2 servings

2	ripe white nectarines
1	apple
1/2 cup	young coconut water or water
1/4 cup	fresh or frozen raspberries

Combine all the ingredients in a blender and process until smooth.

Strawberry Banana Coconut Smoothie

yield: 1–2 servings

2 cups	fresh or frozen strawberries
1	frozen banana
1/2–3/4 cup	young coconut water or water
1/2 cup	young coconut pulp

Combine all the ingredients in a blender and process until smooth.

Tropical Cooler

yield: 1–2 servings

1 large	ripe mango, cut into chunks
1	frozen banana
1 cup	young coconut water
½ cup	young coconut pulp
2 teaspoons	vanilla extract

Combine all the ingredients in a blender and process until smooth.

Breads

The secret to making great bread is in grinding the flaxseeds. Grind the flaxseeds in a coffee grinder or blender. Do not grind the flaxseeds superfine; keep them somewhat coarse and chunky. The bread should be dry and crispy on the outside and firm on the inside. You may need to adjust the time required for dehydrating depending on the weather, the amount of moisture in the ingredients, and your own personal preference. If the dough is dry and crumbly and has difficulty holding together, add a little water.

Apple Cinnamon Bread

yield: 3 loaves

1 cup	almonds, soaked 12–48 hours
1 cup	raisins, soaked 1 hour (reserve soak water)
2 cups	golden flaxseeds, coarsely ground
2	apples, grated
1 tablespoon	ground cinnamon
1 teaspoon	vanilla extract
1 teaspoon	Celtic salt

Process the almonds into a fine meal in a food processor fitted with the S blade. Place the raisins and some of the raisin soak water in a blender and process until smooth. Transfer to a large bowl and stir in the flaxseeds, almonds, apples, cinnamon, vanilla, and salt. Mix well. Form into 3 loaves, each about 4 x 7 x ¾ inches, and dehydrate at 105 degrees for 12–14 hours or until dry and crispy on the outside and firm on the inside.

Apple Zucchini Bread

see photo facing page 281   *yield: 3 loaves*

1 cup	pecans, soaked 1 hour
1 cup	chopped zucchini
½ cup	raisins, soaked 1 hour (reserve soak water)
2 cups	golden flaxseeds, coarsely ground
1	apple, grated
2 teaspoons	ground cinnamon
1 teaspoon	Celtic salt
1 teaspoon	vanilla extract
½ teaspoon	ground nutmeg
¼ teaspoon	ground cardamom

Process the pecans into a fine meal in a food processor fitted with the S blade. Place the zucchini, raisins, and some of the raisin soak water in a blender and process until smooth. Transfer to a large bowl and stir in the ground pecans, flaxseeds, apple, cinnamon, salt, vanilla, nutmeg, and cardamom. Mix well. Form into 3 loaves, each about 4 x 7 x ¾ inches, and dehydrate at 105 degrees for 12–14 hours or until dry and crispy on the outside and firm on the inside.

Breads

Apricot Bread

yield: 3 loaves

1 cup	almonds, soaked 12–48 hours
1 cup	dried apricots, soaked 1 hour (reserve soak water)
2 teaspoons	vanilla extract
2 cups	golden flaxseeds, coarsely ground
1 tablespoon	orange zest
1½ teaspoons	ground cinnamon
1 teaspoon	Celtic salt

Process the almonds into a fine meal in a food processor fitted with the S blade. Place the apricots, vanilla, and some of the apricot soak water in a blender and process until smooth. Transfer to a large bowl and stir in the ground almonds, flaxseeds, orange zest, cinnamon, and salt. Mix well. Form into 3 loaves, each about 4 x 7 x ¾ inches, and dehydrate at 105 degrees for 12–14 hours or until dry and crispy on the outside and firm on the inside.

Blueberry Muffins

yield: 16 muffins

1 cup	cashews, soaked 1 hour
2 cups	golden flaxseeds, coarsely ground
2	apples, grated
1 cup	fresh blueberries, finely chopped
2 teaspoons	vanilla extract
1 teaspoon	Celtic salt

Process the cashews into a fine meal in a food processor fitted with the S blade. Transfer to a large bowl and stir in the flaxseeds, apples, blueberries, vanilla, and salt. Mix well. Form into 16 muffins, each about 2 x ¾ inches. Dehydrate at 105 degrees for 4–6 hours or until dry and crispy on the outside and firm on the inside.

Note: The easiest way to chop the blueberries is in a food processor fitted with the S blade.

Breads

Carrot-Dill Bread

yield: 3 loaves

1 cup	almonds, soaked 12–48 hours
2 cups	golden flaxseeds, coarsely ground
1½ cups	finely grated carrots
1	apple, grated
1 tablespoon	chopped fresh dill weed, or 1 teaspoon dried
1 teaspoon	Celtic salt

*P*rocess the almonds into a fine meal in a food processor fitted with the S blade. Transfer to a large bowl and stir in the flaxseeds, carrots, apple, dill weed, and salt. Mix well. Form into 3 loaves, each about 4 x 7 x ¾ inches, and dehydrate at 105 degrees for 12–14 hours or until dry and crispy on the outside and firm on the inside.

Cranberry Nut Bread

yield: 3 loaves

1 cup	almonds, soaked 12–48 hours
2 cups	golden flaxseeds, coarsely ground
2	apples, grated
1½ cups	fresh cranberries, coarsely chopped
½ cup	walnuts, soaked 1 hour and chopped
2 teaspoons	vanilla extract
1½ teaspoons	ground cinnamon
1 teaspoon	Celtic salt

*P*rocess the almonds into a fine meal in a food processor fitted with the S blade. Transfer to a large bowl and stir in the flaxseeds, apples, cranberries, walnuts, vanilla, cinnamon, and salt. Mix well. Form into 3 loaves, each about 4 x 7 x ¾ inches, and dehydrate at 105 degrees for 12–14 hours or until dry and crispy on the outside and firm on the inside.

Note: The easiest way to chop the cranberries is in a food processor fitted with the S blade.

Focaccia

1 cup	almonds, soaked 12–48 hours
1 large	ripe tomato
2 tablespoons	cold-pressed olive oil
2 tablespoons	finely chopped fresh basil
1 cup	grated apples
2 cups	golden flaxseeds, coarsely ground
1 teaspoon	Celtic salt

Process the almonds into a fine meal in a food processor fitted with the S blade. Combine the tomato, olive oil, and basil in a blender and process until smooth. Transfer to a large bowl and stir in the ground almonds, apples, flaxseeds, and salt. Mix well. Form into 3 loaves, each about 4 x 7 x ¾ inches, and dehydrate at 105 degrees for 12–14 hours or until dry and crispy on the outside and firm on the inside.

Fruit Scones

yield: 16 scones

1 cup	pecans, soaked 1 hour
2 cups	golden flaxseeds, coarsely ground
2	apples, grated
¼ cup	mixed dried fruit (such as pineapple, papaya, and mango)
¼ cup	raisins
¼ cup	shredded dried coconut
1 tablespoon	raw carob powder
1 teaspoon	Celtic salt
1 teaspoon	ground cinnamon

*P*rocess the pecans into a fine meal in a food processor fitted with the S blade. Transfer to a large bowl and stir in the flaxseeds, apples, dried fruit, raisins, coconut, carob powder, salt, and cinnamon. Mix well. Form into 16 scones, each about 2 x ¾ inches. Dehydrate at 105 degrees for 4–6 hours or until dry and crispy on the outside and firm on the inside.

Breads

Herb Seed Bread

yield: 3 loaves

1 cup	pecans, soaked 1 hour
2 cups	golden flaxseeds, coarsely ground
2	apples, grated
1 tablespoon	poppy seeds
1 tablespoon	dried thyme
2 teaspoons	dried rosemary
2 teaspoons	dried sage
1 teaspoon	Celtic salt

Process the pecans into a fine meal in a food processor fitted with the S blade. Transfer to a large bowl and stir in the flaxseeds, apples, poppy seeds, thyme, rosemary, sage, and salt. Mix well. Form into 3 loaves, each about 4 x 7 x ¾ inches, and dehydrate at 105 degrees for 12–14 hours or until dry and crispy on the outside and firm on the inside.

Italian Bread

yield: 3 loaves

1 cup	pecans, soaked 1 hour
2 cups	golden flaxseeds, coarsely ground
2	apples, grated
1 tablespoon	Italian seasoning
1 teaspoon	Celtic salt

*P*rocess the pecans into a fine meal in a food processor fitted with the S blade. Transfer to a large bowl and stir in the flaxseeds, apples, Italian seasoning, and salt. Mix well. Form into 3 loaves, each about 4 x 7 x ¾ inches, and dehydrate at 105 degrees for 12–14 hours or until dry and crispy on the outside and firm on the inside.

Onion Herb Bread

yield: 3 loaves

1 cup	pecans, soaked 1 hour
2 cups	golden flaxseeds, coarsely ground
2	apples, grated
2 teaspoons	onion powder
1 teaspoon	garlic powder
1/2 teaspoon	dried basil
1/2 teaspoon	dried marjoram
1/2 teaspoon	dried summer savory
1/4 teaspoon	dried rosemary
1 teaspoon	Celtic salt

Process the pecans into a fine meal in a food processor fitted with the S blade. Transfer to a large bowl and stir in the flaxseeds, apples, onion powder, garlic powder, basil, marjoram, savory, rosemary, and salt. Mix well. Form into 3 loaves, each about 4 x 7 x 3/4 inches, and dehydrate at 105 degrees for 12–14 hours or until dry and crispy on the outside and firm on the inside.

Pita Bread

yield: 7 (6-inch) pita breads

The thinner you spread the batter, the less time it will take for the pita breads to dehydrate and the better they will taste. To make a perfect circle, cut out the center of a lid to an old plastic storage container to use as a template.

1 cup	golden flaxseeds, soaked 4–6 hours in 1 cup water
½	ripe avocado
½ *cup*	water
½ *teaspoon*	Celtic salt

Combine all the ingredients in a blender and process until smooth. Evenly spread ⅓ cup of the batter on a Teflex sheet, forming a 6-inch circle about ⅛ inch thick. Prepare the remaining batter in the same fashion. Dehydrate at 105 degrees for 3 hours. Flip the bread over, remove the Teflex sheet, and continue dehydrating for 2 hours longer or until the bread is soft and flexible. Remove the bread from the dehydrator when it is slightly crispy. Place it in a zippered plastic bag for several hours and it will become more flexible. For the best results, dehydrate the bread the night before you plan to use it.

Breads

Pumpkin Bread

yield: 3 loaves

1 cup	pecans, soaked 1 hour
1 cup	chopped fresh pumpkin
2 cups	golden flaxseeds, coarsely ground
1	apple, grated
2 teaspoons	ground cinnamon
1 teaspoon	ground ginger
1 teaspoon	Celtic salt
1 teaspoon	vanilla extract
¼ teaspoon	ground cloves

Process the pecans into a fine meal in a food processor fitted with the S blade. Transfer to a large bowl. Blend the pumpkin in a food processor or blender until smooth, adding a small amount of water if needed to facilitate processing. Stir into the pecans and add the flaxseeds, apple, cinnamon, ginger, salt, vanilla, and cloves. Mix well. Form into 3 loaves, each about 4 x 7 x ¾ inches, and dehydrate at 105 degrees for 12–14 hours or until dry and crispy on the outside and firm on the inside.

Photo: Chiles Rellenos, page 216

Sun-Dried Tomato Bread

yield: 3 loaves

1 cup	pecans, soaked 1 hour
½ cup	sun-dried tomatoes, soaked 2 hours (reserve soak water)
2 cups	golden flaxseeds, coarsely ground
2	apples, grated
1 tablespoon	finely chopped fresh basil
1 tablespoon	finely chopped fresh oregano
1 teaspoon	Celtic salt

*P*rocess the pecans into a fine meal in a food processor fitted with the S blade. Transfer to a large bowl. Place the tomatoes in a blender with some of their soak water and process until smooth. Stir into the pecans along with the flaxseeds, apples, basil, oregano, and salt. Mix well. Form into 3 loaves, each about 4 x 7 x ¾ inches, and dehydrate at 105 degrees for 12–14 hours or until dry and crispy on the outside and firm on the inside.

Photo: Asian Spinach Salad, page 140, Stuffed Tomatoes, page 234

Breads

Walnut Scones

yield: 16 scones

1 cup	cashews, soaked 1 hour
2 cups	golden flaxseeds, coarsely ground
2	apples, grated
1 cup	walnuts, soaked 2 hours and chopped
½ cup	raisins
2 teaspoons	ground cinnamon
2 teaspoons	vanilla extract
1 teaspoon	Celtic salt
⅛ teaspoon	ground nutmeg

*P*rocess the cashews into a fine meal in a food processor fitted with the S blade. Transfer to a large bowl and stir in the flaxseeds, apples, walnuts, raisins, cinnamon, vanilla, salt, and nutmeg. Mix well. Form into 16 scones, each about 2 x ¾ inches. Dehydrate at 105 degrees for 4–6 hours or until dry and crispy on the outside and firm on the inside.

Zucchini Pineapple Bread

yield: 3 loaves

1 cup	pecans, soaked 1 hour
1½ cups	raisins, soaked 4–6 hours (reserve soak water)
1 cup	zucchini
2 cups	golden flaxseeds, coarsely ground
¼ cup	dried pineapple, finely chopped
2 teaspoons	ground cinnamon
1 teaspoon	vanilla extract
1 teaspoon	Celtic salt

*P*rocess the pecans into a fine meal in a food processor fitted with the S blade. Transfer to a large bowl. Combine the raisins and zucchini in a food processor and process until smooth, adding some of the raisin soak water as needed. Stir into the ground pecans along with the flaxseeds, pineapple, cinnamon, vanilla, and salt. Mix well. Form into 3 loaves, each about 4 x 7 x ¾ inches, and dehydrate at 105 degrees for 12–14 hours or until dry and crispy on the outside and firm on the inside.

Crackers

Moistening your hands with water will help the batter spread more easily. It is important to dehydrate the crackers until all the moisture is removed. Crackers will keep for up to six months if properly dehydrated and stored in glass jars.

Almond Flax Crackers

yield: 9 trays, 14 x 14 inches each

4 cups	almonds, soaked 12–48 hours
4 cups	carrot pulp with juice
6 cups	brown flaxseeds, soaked 4–6 hours in 6 cups water
2 cups	finely chopped fresh parsley
1 cup	pumpkin seeds, soaked 8 hours
1 cup	sesame seeds, soaked 8 hours
6	celery stalks, finely chopped
6 tablespoons	fresh lemon juice
3 tablespoons	Celtic salt
3 tablespoons	kelp powder

Process the almonds and carrots through a Champion Juicer with the solid plate. Transfer to a large bowl and stir in the flaxseeds, parsley, pumpkin seeds, sesame seeds, celery, lemon juice, salt, and kelp. Mix well. Spread ¼ inch thick on a dehydrator tray with a Teflex sheet. Score the crackers with a knife. Prepare the remaining mixture in the same fashion. Dehydrate at 105 degrees for 6 hours. Turn over, remove the Teflex sheet, and continue dehydrating for 6–8 hours longer or until the desired crispness is achieved. Store in glass jars.

Crackers

Autumn Crackers

yield: 9 trays, 14 x 14 inches each

4 cups	pumpkin pulp with juice
2½ cups	carrot pulp with juice
2 cups	almonds, soaked 12–48 hours
4 cups	brown flaxseeds, soaked 4–6 hours in 4 cups water
1 large	red onion, finely chopped
1 large	red bell pepper, finely chopped
1 cup	finely chopped fresh cilantro
4 teaspoons	ground cumin
1 tablespoon	Celtic salt

Process the pumpkin, carrots, and almonds through a Champion Juicer with the solid plate. Transfer to a large bowl and stir in the flaxseeds, onion, bell pepper, cilantro, cumin, and salt. Mix well. Spread ¼ inch thick on a dehydrator tray with a Teflex sheet. Score the crackers with a knife. Prepare the remaining mixture in the same fashion. Dehydrate at 105 degrees for 6 hours. Turn over, remove the Teflex sheet, and continue dehydrating for 6–8 hours longer or until the desired crispness is achieved. Store in glass jars.

Carrot and Seed Crackers

yield: 9 trays, 14 x 14 inches each

8 cups	brown flaxseeds, soaked 4–6 hours in 8 cups water
4 cups	carrot pulp with juice
1 cup	beet pulp
1 cup	fresh celery juice
1 cup	pumpkin seeds, soaked 8 hours
1 cup	sesame seeds, soaked 8 hours
1 cup	sunflower seeds, soaked 6–8 hours
1	red onion, finely chopped
3 tablespoons	Celtic salt

Combine all the ingredients in a large bowl and mix well. Spread ¼ inch thick on a dehydrator tray with a Teflex sheet. Score the crackers with a knife. Prepare the remaining mixture in the same fashion. Dehydrate at 105 degrees for 5–6 hours. Turn over, remove the Teflex sheet, and continue dehydrating for 5–6 hours longer or until the crackers are completely dry. Store in glass jars.

Corn Chips

yield: 25 chips

6	ears corn, kernels removed
1/2	yellow onion, chopped
2 cups	sunflower seeds, soaked 6–8 hours and rinsed
1/4 cup	water as needed
1/4 cup	golden flaxseeds, finely ground
1 teaspoon	Celtic salt
1/2 teaspoon	onion powder
1/4 teaspoon	cayenne

Combine the kernels and onion in a food processor fitted with the S blade and process until smooth, stopping as needed to scrape down the sides of the work bowl. Add the sunflower seeds and process until the mixture is well blended and has the consistency of a batter. Add a little water if the batter seems too thick. Stir in the flaxseeds, salt, onion powder, and cayenne and mix well. Using a teaspoon, scoop the batter onto a dehydrator tray with a Teflex sheet. Flatten with a table knife into a thin round, about 1/8 inch thick and 1 1/2 inches wide. Prepare the remaining batter in the same fashion. Dehydrate at 105 degrees for 12 hours. Turn the chips over and remove the Teflex sheet. Continue dehydrating for 10–12 hours or until the desired crispness is achieved. Store in glass jars.

Fiesta Crackers with Lime Juice

yield: 7 trays, 14 x 14 inches each

6 cups	brown flaxseeds, soaked 4–6 hours in 7 cups water
3 cups	carrot pulp with juice
1½ cups	finely chopped fresh cilantro
1½ cups	finely chopped white onions
⅔ cup	fresh lime juice
2 tablespoons	Celtic salt
1 teaspoon	cayenne

Combine all the ingredients in a large bowl and mix well. Spread ¼ inch thick on a dehydrator tray with a Teflex sheet. Score the crackers with a knife. Prepare the remaining mixture in the same fashion. Dehydrate at 105 degrees for 5–6 hours. Turn over, remove the Teflex sheet, and continue dehydrating for 5–6 hours longer or until the crackers are completely dry. Store in glass jars.

Crackers

Italian Crackers

yield: 4 trays, 14 x 14 inches each

2 cups	pecans, soaked 1 hour
2	zucchini
2 cups	brown flaxseeds, soaked 4–6 hours in 2 cups water
2 tablespoons	Italian seasoning
1 tablespoon	Celtic salt

Process the pecans and zucchini through a Champion Juicer with the solid plate. Transfer to a large bowl and stir in the flaxseeds, Italian seasoning, and salt and mix well. Keep the mixture moist and loose. Spread ¼ inch thick on a dehydrator tray with a Teflex sheet. Score the crackers with a knife. Prepare the remaining mixture in the same fashion. Dehydrate at 105 degrees for 5–6 hours. Turn over, remove the Teflex sheet, and continue dehydrating for 4–5 hours longer or until the crackers are completely dry. Store in glass jars.

Italian Sun-Dried Tomato Flax Crackers

yield: 4 trays, 14 x 14 inches each

4 cups	brown flaxseeds, soaked 4–6 hours in 4 cups water
2 cups	sun-dried tomatoes, soaked 4 hours and blended
2 tablespoons	Italian seasoning
1 tablespoon	cold-pressed olive oil
1 tablespoon	Celtic salt

Combine all the ingredients in a large bowl and mix well. Spread ¼ inch thick on a dehydrator tray with a Teflex sheet. Score the crackers with a knife. Prepare the remaining mixture in the same fashion. Dehydrate at 105 degrees for 5–6 hours. Turn over, remove the Teflex sheet, and continue dehydrating for 5–6 hours longer or until the crackers are completely dry. Store in glass jars.

Crackers

Mexican Flax Crackers

yield: 9 trays, 14 x 14 inches each

see photo facing

page 281

4 cups	carrot pulp with juice
3 cups	almonds, soaked 12–48 hours
6 cups	golden flaxseeds, soaked 4–6 hours in 6 cups water
1 cup	finely chopped fresh cilantro
4	celery stalks, finely chopped
1	red bell pepper, finely chopped
1	red onion, finely chopped
1/4 cup	fresh lemon juice
2 tablespoons	Celtic salt
1/2 teaspoon	cayenne

Process the carrots and almonds through a Champion Juicer with the solid plate. Transfer to a large bowl and stir in the remaining ingredients. Mix well. Spread 1/4 inch thick on a dehydrator tray with a Teflex sheet. Score the crackers with a knife. Prepare the remaining mixture in the same fashion. Dehydrate at 105 degrees for 6 hours. Turn over, remove the Teflex sheet, and continue dehydrating for 6–8 hours longer or until the desired crispness is achieved. Store in glass jars.

Nori Sesame Crackers

yield: 54 crackers

2 cups	almonds, soaked 12–48 hours
1 cup	sunflower seeds, soaked 4–6 hours and rinsed
1/4 cup	finely chopped fresh basil, or 2 teaspoons dried
1/4 cup	finely chopped fresh parsley, or 2 teaspoons dried
1 tablespoon	finely chopped fresh rosemary, or 1 teaspoon dried
1–2	garlic cloves
1/4 cup	raw tahini
2 tablespoons	fresh lemon juice
1/4 teaspoon	cayenne
6	nori sheets
1/2 cup	sesame seeds, soaked 6–8 hours and rinsed

Process the almonds, sunflower seeds, basil, parsley, rosemary, and garlic through a Champion Juicer with the solid plate, or in a food processor fitted with the S blade. Transfer to a large bowl and stir in the tahini, lemon juice, and cayenne and mix well. Spread the batter 1/8 inch thick on the nori sheets. Sprinkle the top with the sesame seeds, and score each sheet into 9 crackers before dehydrating (do not cut through the nori). Place on a dehydrator tray with a mesh screen. Dehydrate at 105 degrees for 15–20 hours or until the desired crispness is achieved. Store in glass jars.

Seed Crackers with Lemon Juice

yield: 7 trays, 14 x 14 inches each

6 cups	brown flaxseeds, soaked 4–6 hours in 7 cups water
3 cups	carrot pulp with juice
1½ cups	finely chopped fresh parsley
1½ cups	finely chopped red onions
1 cup	pumpkin seeds, soaked 6–8 hours
1 cup	sunflower seeds, soaked 4–6 hours
⅔ cup	fresh lemon juice
2 tablespoons	Celtic salt

Combine all the ingredients in a large bowl and mix well. Spread ¼ inch thick on a dehydrator tray with a Teflex sheet. Score the crackers with a knife. Prepare the remaining mixture in the same fashion. Dehydrate at 105 degrees for 5–6 hours. Turn over, remove the Teflex sheet, and continue dehydrating for 5–6 hours longer or until the crackers are completely dry. Store in glass jars.

Taste of India Flaxseed Crackers

yield: 7 trays, 14 x 14 inches each

4 cups	carrot pulp with juice
3 cups	almonds, soaked 12–48 hours
4 cups	brown flaxseeds, soaked 4–6 hours in 6 cups water
4	celery stalks, finely chopped
1 large	red onion, finely chopped
1½ cups	finely chopped fresh parsley
½ cup	cold-pressed olive oil
¼ cup	fresh lemon juice
3 tablespoons	Celtic salt
1 tablespoon	curry powder
2–4	garlic cloves, finely chopped
2 teaspoons	ground cumin
2 teaspoons	ground ginger
1 teaspoon	ground coriander

Process the carrots and almonds through a Champion Juicer with the solid plate. Transfer to a large bowl and stir in the remaining ingredients. Mix well. Spread ¼ inch thick on a dehydrator tray with a Teflex sheet. Score the crackers with a knife. Prepare the remaining mixture in the same fashion. Dehydrate at 105 degrees for 6 hours. Turn over, remove the Teflex sheet, and continue dehydrating for 6–8 hours longer or until the desired crispness is achieved. Store in glass jars.

Walnut Crackers

yield: 3 trays, 14 x 14 inches each

2 cups	walnuts, soaked 4 hours
2	apples, chopped
½ cup	raisins, soaked 2 hours in ½ cup water (reserve soak water)
3 cups	brown flaxseeds, soaked 4–6 hours in 3 cups water
2 teaspoons	vanilla extract
1½ teaspoons	ground cinnamon
1 teaspoon	Celtic salt

Process the walnuts through a Champion Juicer with the solid plate, or in a food processor fitted with the S blade. Transfer to a large bowl. Place the apples, raisins, and raisin soak water in a blender and process until smooth. Stir into the walnuts along with the flaxseeds, vanilla, cinnamon, and salt. Mix well. Spread ¼ inch thick on a dehydrator tray with a Teflex sheet. Score the crackers with a knife. Prepare the remaining mixture in the same fashion. Dehydrate at 105 degrees for 6 hours. Turn over, remove the Teflex sheet, and continue dehydrating for 8–10 hours longer or until the desired crispness is achieved. Store in glass jars.

Appetizers

Apple Salsa

yield: 3–4 cups

3	Fuji apples, finely chopped
2	red bell peppers, finely chopped
1 cup	finely chopped red onions
¼ cup	fresh lime juice
2 tablespoons	finely chopped fresh cilantro
1 tablespoon	cold-pressed olive oil
1 tablespoon	raw apple cider vinegar
1	garlic clove, finely chopped
1	jalapeño chile, seeded and finely chopped
½ teaspoon	Celtic salt

Combine all the ingredients in a bowl and mix well.

Corn and Garlic Salsa

yield: 3 cups

3	ripe tomatoes, finely chopped
2 cups	fresh corn kernels
¼ cup	finely chopped fresh cilantro
¼ cup	fresh lime juice
2 tablespoons	cold-pressed olive oil
1	jalapeño chile, seeded and finely chopped
1–2	garlic cloves, thinly sliced
½ teaspoon	Celtic salt

Combine all the ingredients in a bowl and mix well. Let stand for 1 hour at room temperature so the flavors can develop.

Appetizers

Fresh Tomato Salsa

yield: 2 cups

3 large	ripe tomatoes, diced
½	red bell pepper, finely chopped
½ cup	finely chopped red onions
2 tablespoons	finely chopped fresh cilantro
2 tablespoons	finely chopped fresh parsley
2 tablespoons	fresh lime juice
½	jalapeño chile, seeded and finely chopped
1 small	garlic clove, minced
¼ teaspoon	Celtic salt

Combine all the ingredients in a bowl and mix well.

Guacamole

yield: 4–6 cups

4	ripe tomatoes, chopped
3–4	hot green chiles, seeded and finely chopped
1 cup	finely chopped red onions
½ cup	finely chopped fresh cilantro
2 tablespoons	fresh lime juice
¼ teaspoon	Celtic salt
6	ripe avocados
	Sprigs of fresh cilantro for garnish

Combine the tomatoes, chiles, onions, cilantro, lime juice, and salt in a bowl. In a separate bowl, mash the avocados and stir into the tomato mixture. Garnish with sprigs of fresh cilantro.

Guacamole Supreme

yield: 2 cups

1	ripe tomato, chopped
¼ cup	finely chopped fresh cilantro
¼ cup	minced white onions
1–2	garlic cloves, minced
1 tablespoon	fresh lime juice
1 very small	jalapeño chile, seeded and finely chopped
⅛ teaspoon	Celtic salt
3	ripe avocados

Combine the tomato, cilantro, onions, garlic, lime juice, chile, and salt in a bowl. In a separate bowl, mash the avocados and stir into the tomato mixture.

Middle Eastern Spicy Almonds

yield: 2 cups

This is a great recipe to double or even triple. Just be sure the almonds are completely dry so they don't mold.

2 cups	almonds, soaked 12–48 hours
1 tablespoon	flax oil or cold-pressed olive oil
1 teaspoon	ground coriander
1 teaspoon	ground cumin
1 teaspoon	garlic powder
1 teaspoon	onion powder
¼ teaspoon	Celtic salt
⅛ teaspoon	cayenne

Dry the almonds with a towel to remove excess moisture. Place in a bowl and add the remaining ingredients. Mix well. Arrange on a dehydrator tray with a Teflex sheet, and dehydrate at 105 degrees for 18–24 hours. The almonds should be completely dry and crunchy. Store in glass jars.

Appetizers

Mixed Honey Nuts

yield: 2 cups

This recipe is great for backpacking. Keep some in the car for whenever hunger strikes.

½ cup	almonds, soaked 12–48 hours
½ cup	pecans, soaked 1 hour
½ cup	cashews, soaked 1 hour
½ cup	pistachios, soaked 1 hour
1 tablespoon	flax oil
1 tablespoon	raw honey (see note)
1 teaspoon	ground cinnamon
½ teaspoon	Celtic salt

Dry the nuts with a towel to remove excess moisture. Combine the nuts in a bowl and add the remaining ingredients. Mix well. Arrange on a dehydrator tray with a Teflex sheet, and dehydrate at 105 degrees for 10 hours. Remove the Teflex sheet and continue dehydrating for 8–14 hours longer. Store in glass jars.

Note: If the nuts are not sweet enough for your taste, add an additional tablespoon of honey.

Onion Rings

yield: 1–2 servings

¹⁄₂ cup	ground brown flaxseeds
2 tablespoons	dried parsley
¹⁄₂ teaspoon	garlic powder
¹⁄₄ teaspoon	Celtic salt
1 very large	sweet onion (such as Walla Walla)

Combine the flaxseeds, parsley, garlic powder, and salt in a small bowl. Slice the onion into ¹⁄₄-inch-thick rounds. Coat each round with the flaxseed mixture and arrange the slices on a dehydrator tray. Dehydrate at 105 degrees for 18–24 hours or until the desired dryness is achieved.

Appetizers

Spicy Mixed Nuts

yield: 5 cups

1 cup	almonds, soaked 12–48 hours
1 cup	pecans, soaked 1 hour
1 cup	pumpkin seeds, soaked 4–6 hours
1 cup	sunflower seeds, soaked 4–6 hours
1 cup	walnuts, soaked 1 hour
2 tablespoons	cold-pressed olive oil
1 tablespoon	curry powder
2 teaspoons	garlic powder
2 teaspoons	onion powder
1 teaspoon	Celtic salt
¼ teaspoon	cayenne

Dry the nuts with a towel to remove excess moisture. Combine the nuts in a bowl and add the remaining ingredients. Mix well. Arrange on a dehydrator tray and dehydrate at 105 degrees for 18–24 hours or until the desired dryness is achieved. Store in glass jars.

Note: It is important that all the moisture is removed from the nuts if they are going to be stored; otherwise they may mold.

Spicy Sunflower Seeds

yield: 2 cups

2 cups	sunflower seeds, soaked 4–6 hours
1 tablespoon	cold-pressed olive oil
1 teaspoon	garlic powder
1 teaspoon	ground ginger
1/2 teaspoon	Celtic salt
Pinch	cayenne

Dry the seeds with a towel to remove excess moisture. Place in a large bowl and add the remaining ingredients. Mix well. Arrange on a dehydrator tray and dehydrate at 105 degrees for 18–24 hours or until the desired dryness is achieved. Store in glass jars.

Note: It is important that all the moisture is removed from the seeds if they are going to be stored; otherwise they may mold.

Appetizers

Stuffed Celery

Celery stalks
Raw almond butter or other nut butter of your choice

Stuff the stalks with the nut butter and serve.

Stuffed Dates

Pitted medjool dates
Raw almond butter or other nut butter of your choice

Stuff the dates with the nut butter and serve.

Pâtés

Pâtés taste best and have a better texture when they are made in a Champion Juicer. However, a food processor will work in a pinch if it is the only equipment available. To make pâtés in a food processor, add ¼ to ½ cup of water and process the nuts until they are smooth and creamy.

Best Ever Almond Pâté

yield: 4 cups

2 cups	almonds, soaked 12–48 hours
3	carrots
1 cup	sunflower seeds, soaked 4–6 hours
3	celery stalks, finely chopped
1	red bell pepper, finely chopped
½	red onion, finely chopped
½ cup	finely chopped fresh parsley
2 tablespoons	fresh lemon juice
1 teaspoon	Celtic salt
¼ teaspoon	cayenne, or 1–2 teaspoons curry powder (optional)

Process the almonds, carrots, and sunflower seeds through a Champion Juicer with the solid plate, or in a food processor fitted with the S blade. Transfer to a large bowl and stir in the remaining ingredients. Mix well.

Carrot Pâté

yield: 4 cups

2 cups	almonds, soaked 12–48 hours
4	carrots, finely grated
3	celery stalks, finely chopped
½ cup	finely chopped red onions
¼ cup	fresh lemon juice
2 tablespoons	kelp powder
1 teaspoon	Celtic salt

*P*rocess the almonds through a Champion Juicer with the solid plate, or in a food processor fitted with the S blade until smooth and creamy. Transfer to a large bowl and stir in the remaining ingredients. Mix well.

Carrot Dill Pâté

yield: 4 cups

2 cups	almonds, soaked 12–48 hours
2	carrots
½ cup	finely chopped fresh dill weed
¼ cup	fresh lemon juice
1 teaspoon	Celtic salt

*P*rocess the almonds and carrots through a Champion Juicer with the solid plate, or in a food processor fitted with the S blade. Transfer to a bowl and stir in the remaining ingredients. Mix well.

Pâtés

Cheese Spread

yield: 4 *cups*

2 cups	almonds, soaked 12–48 hours
1/4 cup	water
1	red bell pepper
2	celery stalks, finely chopped
1/2 cup	finely chopped fresh parsley
2 tablespoons	fresh lemon juice
2 tablespoons	nutritional yeast
1 teaspoon	Celtic salt

Finely chop the almonds in a food processor fitted with the S blade. Slowly add the water and process for 2–3 minutes until smooth. Add the red bell pepper and process until smooth and creamy. Transfer to a bowl and stir in the remaining ingredients. Mix well.

Curry Pâté

yield: 4 cups

2 cups	almonds, soaked 12–48 hours
3	celery stalks, finely chopped
1	carrot, finely grated
½ cup	finely chopped leeks
½ cup	finely chopped fresh parsley
2 tablespoons	fresh lemon juice
1–2 teaspoons	curry powder
1 teaspoon	Celtic salt

Process the almonds through a Champion Juicer with the solid plate, or in a food processor fitted with the S blade until smooth and creamy. Transfer to a bowl and stir in the remaining ingredients. Mix well.

Pâtés

Hummus

yield: 2 *cups*

1 cup	almonds, soaked 12–48 hours
¹/₂–³/₄	cup water as needed
³/₄ *cup*	sesame seeds, soaked 6–8 hours
3 tablespoons	fresh lemon juice
1 tablespoon	cold-pressed olive oil
1¹/₂ teaspoons	ground cumin
³/₄ *teaspoon*	Celtic salt
1–2	garlic cloves
	Minced fresh parsley for garnish

Finely chop the almonds in a food processor fitted with the S blade. Slowly add ¼ cup of the water and process for 2–3 minutes until creamy. Transfer to a blender along with ¼ cup of the remaining water, the sesame seeds, lemon juice, olive oil, cumin, salt, and garlic. Process until smooth, adding a little more of the water if needed to facilitate blending. Garnish with the parsley.

Nut and Seed Pâté

yield: 4 cups

1 cup	almonds, soaked 12–48 hours
1 cup	pumpkin seeds, soaked 8 hours
1 cup	sunflower seeds, soaked 4–6 hours and rinsed
1 cup	finely chopped fresh parsley
2	celery stalks, finely chopped
2 tablespoons	fresh lemon juice
1 teaspoon	Celtic salt
1 teaspoon	kelp powder
1–2	garlic cloves, pressed

Process the almonds, pumpkin seeds, and sunflower seeds through a Champion Juicer with the solid plate, or in a food processor fitted with the S blade. Transfer to a bowl and stir in the remaining ingredients. Mix well.

Pecan Pâté

yield: 4 cups

2 cups	pecans, soaked 4 hours
2 cups	finely chopped celery
½ cup	finely chopped leeks
2 tablespoons	fresh lemon juice
2 teaspoons	ground cumin
2 teaspoons	kelp powder
1 teaspoon	Celtic salt

Process the pecans through a Champion Juicer with the solid plate, or in a food processor fitted with the S blade. Transfer to a bowl and stir in the remaining ingredients. Mix well.

Refried "Bean" Pâté

yield: 3 cups

2 cups	almonds, soaked 12–48 hours
1 cup	sun-dried tomatoes, soaked 2–4 hours
1 tablespoon	Mexican seasoning
2 teaspoons	fresh lemon juice (optional)
1½ tablespoons	raw red miso (optional)
1 teaspoon	Celtic salt

Combine all the ingredients in a food processor fitted with the S blade and process until smooth and creamy. If necessary, add a small amount of water to facilitate blending.

Sun-Dried Tomato Pâté

yield: 2¹/₂ cups

2 cups	almonds, soaked 12–48 hours
¹/₂ cup	sun-dried tomatoes, soaked 4 hours
2 tablespoons	finely chopped fresh basil
2 tablespoons	fresh lemon juice
1 teaspoon	Italian seasoning
1 teaspoon	Celtic salt
1–2	garlic cloves, minced

Process the almonds and sun-dried tomatoes through a Champion Juicer with the solid plate, or in a food processor fitted with the S blade. Transfer to a bowl and stir in the remaining ingredients. Mix well.

Sunny Hazelnut Pâté

yield: 4 *cups*

1½ cups	sunflower seeds, soaked 4–6 hours and rinsed
1 cup	almonds, soaked 12–48 hours
1 cup	hazelnuts, soaked 6 hours
4	carrots, finely shredded
½	red onion, finely chopped
2	celery stalks, finely chopped
2 tablespoons	fresh lemon juice
1 teaspoon	Celtic salt
1 teaspoon	kelp powder

Process the sunflower seeds, almonds, and hazelnuts through a Champion Juicer with the solid plate, or in a food processor fitted with the S blade. Transfer to a bowl and stir in the remaining ingredients. Mix well.

Pâtés

Tastes Fishy

This recipe is one of my favorites.

2 cups	almonds, soaked 12–48 hours
1 cup	finely chopped fresh parsley
4	celery stalks, finely chopped
1/2 cup	finely chopped red onions
1/4 cup	fresh lemon juice
2 teaspoons	kelp powder
1 teaspoon	Celtic salt

Process the almonds through a Champion Juicer with the solid plate, or in a food processor fitted with the S blade. Transfer to a bowl and stir in the remaining ingredients. Mix well.

Taste of India

yield: 2½ cups

3	carrots
1 cup	almonds, soaked 12–48 hours
1 cup	sunflower seeds, soaked 4–6 hours and rinsed
½	red onion, finely chopped
2	celery stalks, finely chopped
1 tablespoon	fresh lemon juice
1 teaspoon	curry powder
1 teaspoon	kelp powder
1 teaspoon	Celtic salt
½ teaspoon	ground coriander
½ teaspoon	ground ginger

Process the carrots, almonds, and sunflower seeds through a Champion Juicer with the solid plate, or in a food processor fitted with the S blade. Transfer to a bowl and stir in the remaining ingredients. Mix well.

Walnut Pâté

yield: 4 cups

2 cups	walnuts, soaked 2 hours
1/2 cup	pine nuts, soaked 1 hour
1/4 cup	water
2	celery stalks, finely chopped
1/4 cup	finely chopped Italian parsley
1/4 cup	finely chopped leeks
1 teaspoon	Italian seasoning
1 teaspoon	Celtic salt

Process the walnuts and pine nuts into a fine meal in a food processor fitted with the S blade. Add the water and process until smooth, creamy, and thick. Transfer to a bowl and stir in the remaining ingredients. Mix well.

Soups

When preparing raw soups, some blenders will warm the ingredients as they are being processed. This is particularly beneficial if you want a lightly warmed soup. Alternatively, raw soups may be gently warmed on the stovetop. As long as you keep the temperature under 120 degrees, you can still enjoy a warm soup that is rich in enzymes and nutrition. Raw soups are also wonderful served cold. A bowl of cold soup is incredibly refreshing on a warm summer afternoon.

Pea Soup

yield: 2–3 servings

2 *cups*	fresh peas
2 *cups*	water
1	ripe avocado
6	fresh basil leaves, finely chopped (optional)
1 *teaspoon*	Celtic salt
½ *teaspoon*	onion powder or garlic powder

Combine all the ingredients in a blender and process until smooth and creamy.

Corny Carrot Soup

yield: 4 servings

2	ears corn, kernels removed
1	ripe avocado
4 *cups*	fresh carrot juice
1 *tablespoon*	grated fresh ginger
1 *teaspoon*	Celtic salt

Combine the corn kernels and avocado in a food processor fitted with the S blade and process until well combined but slightly chunky. Add the carrot juice, ginger, and salt and process for 30 seconds.

Carrot Fennel Soup

yield: 4 servings

4 cups	water
2 cups	chopped carrots
1	ripe avocado
1	apple, chopped
1	fennel bulb, chopped
2 tablespoons	fresh dill weed
1 teaspoon	Celtic salt

Combine all the ingredients in a blender and process until smooth and creamy. If the soup is too thick, add a little carrot juice to achieve the desired consistency.

French Onion Mushroom Soup

yield: 4 servings

2½–3 cups	water
1 cup	almonds, soaked 12–48 hours
½ cup	cashews, soaked 1 hour
1¼ cup	shiitake mushrooms
2	celery stalks, chopped
1 teaspoon	Celtic salt
1 teaspoon	dried tarragon
½ teaspoon	onion powder
¼ teaspoon	garlic powder

Combine the water, almonds, and cashews in a blender and process until smooth and creamy. Add the shiitake mushrooms, celery, salt, tarragon, onion powder, and garlic powder and process until smooth.

Nori Soup

yield: 1–2 servings

1½ cups	warm water (under 120 degrees)
2	nori sheets, cut into ¼-inch strips
1 tablespoon	finely chopped scallions or chives
½ teaspoon	fresh lemon juice
½ teaspoon	Nama Shoyu
Pinch	Celtic salt
	Fresh lemongrass or ginger (optional)

Combine all the ingredients in a saucepan, adding the optional lemongrass or ginger to taste. Warm on the stove on the lowest setting (120 degrees or lower) for 10–15 minutes. Serve warm.

Soups

Nori Dulse Soup

yield: 2–4 servings

3–4 cups	water
1	nori sheet
½ cup	dulse, rinsed
½ cup	raw tahini
1 tablespoon	grated fresh ginger
1–2	garlic cloves, minced
1 cup	chopped mung bean sprouts
1 cup	finely chopped baby spinach
½ cup	finely chopped shiitake mushrooms
3	scallions, finely chopped
¼ cup	chopped pine nuts, soaked 1 hour
¼ teaspoon	Celtic salt

Combine the water, nori, dulse, tahini, ginger, and garlic in a blender and process until smooth. Stir in the sprouts, spinach, mushrooms, scallions, pine nuts, and salt and mix well.

Sweet China Soup

yield: 2–4 servings

2 cups	water
2 cups	sunflower sprouts
2	apples (such as Fuji), chopped
2	carrots, chopped
2	celery stalks, chopped
1/2	ripe avocado
1/2 small	beet
2 tablespoons	fresh lemon juice
2 tablespoons	unpasteurized miso
1/2 teaspoon	Chinese five-spice

Combine all the ingredients in a blender and process until smooth and creamy.

Soups

Tomato Soup

yield: 2–4 servings

see photo facing page 281

4	ripe tomatoes
2	carrots
1	ripe avocado
1	cucumber
¼ cup	chopped fresh parsley
1 tablespoon	fresh lemon juice
1 teaspoon	Celtic salt
	Freshly ground pepper

Combine all the ingredients in a blender and process until smooth and creamy.

Tomato Basil Soup

yield: 2–3 servings

4	ripe tomatoes
2	celery stalks
1/4 cup	sun-dried tomatoes, soaked 1 hour in 3/4 cup water (reserve soak water)
1/4 cup	finely chopped fresh basil
1 tablespoon	fresh oregano, or 1 teaspoon dried
1/2 teaspoon	Italian seasoning
1/2 teaspoon	Celtic salt

Combine the fresh tomatoes, celery, sun-dried tomatoes, tomato soak water, basil, oregano, Italian seasoning, and salt in a blender and process until smooth and creamy.

Tomato Fennel Soup

yield: 2–3 servings

2 cups	chopped fennel bulbs
1 cup	chopped ripe tomatoes
2 tablespoons	fresh lemon juice
1 teaspoon	Italian seasoning
½ teaspoon	Celtic salt
1–2	garlic cloves
½ cup	diced ripe avocado
½ cup	diced cucumbers
⅓ cup	diced red bell peppers
	Fresh herbs (such as basil, oregano, dill weed, or fennel) for garnish

Combine the fennel, tomatoes, lemon juice, Italian seasoning, salt, and garlic in a blender and process until smooth. Stir in the avocado, cucumbers, and red bell peppers. Garnish with the fresh herbs.

Salads

Arabian Mixed Green Salad

yield: 1–2 servings

4 cups	mixed greens
2	ripe tomatoes, cut into wedges
1 cup	fresh mint
1 cup	watercress leaves, stems removed
1/2 cup	finely chopped scallions
5 tablespoons	sesame oil
3 tablespoons	fresh lemon juice
1/4 teaspoon	Celtic salt
	Freshly ground pepper

Combine the greens, tomatoes, mint, watercress, and scallions in a bowl. Place the sesame oil, lemon juice, salt, and pepper to taste in a jar. Seal tightly and shake well. Pour over the vegetables and toss gently.

Arabian Parsley-Sesame Salad

yield: 3–4 servings

2 bunches	parsley, finely chopped
⅓ cup	raw tahini
¼ cup	fresh lemon juice
2 tablespoons	cold-pressed olive oil
2–3	garlic cloves, minced
¼ teaspoon	Celtic salt
¼ teaspoon	cayenne
	Large lettuce leaves
	Sunflower sprouts

Combine the parsley, tahini, lemon juice, olive oil, garlic, salt, and cayenne in a bowl. Stir well to make a thick sauce. Spoon over the lettuce leaves and top with the sunflower sprouts.

Arugula and Tomato Salad

4 cups	baby arugula
2	ripe tomatoes, cut into thin wedges
2 tablespoons	cold-pressed olive oil
2 tablespoons	fresh lemon juice
¼ teaspoon	Celtic salt

Combine all the ingredients in a large bowl and mix well.

Arugula and Watercress Salad

yield: 2–4 servings

4 cups	arugula
2 cups	watercress
½ cup	finely chopped red onions
½ cup	ripe cherry tomatoes, halved
2 tablespoons	cold-pressed olive oil
1 tablespoon	raw apple cider vinegar
1 tablespoon	dry mustard
1 tablespoon	fresh orange juice
2 teaspoons	orange zest
¼ teaspoon	Celtic salt
2 tablespoons	sesame seeds for garnish

Combine the arugula, watercress, onions, and cherry tomatoes in a large bowl. Place the olive oil, vinegar, dry mustard, orange juice, orange zest, and salt in a jar. Seal tightly and shake well. Pour over the vegetables and toss gently. Garnish with the sesame seeds.

Arugula with Apple-Fennel Salad

yield: 2–4 servings

6 cups	arugula
2	apples, thinly sliced
1	fennel bulb, julienned
¼ cup	julienned red onions
¼ cup	cold-pressed olive oil
2 tablespoons	fresh lemon juice
¼ teaspoon	Celtic salt

Combine all the ingredients in a large bowl and mix well.

Arugula with Pine Nut Dressing

yield: 2–4 servings

6 cups	baby arugula
2	ripe tomatoes, cut into thin wedges
½ cup	finely chopped red onions
¼ teaspoon	Celtic salt
⅓ cup	finely chopped fresh parsley
¼ cup	cold-pressed olive oil
¼ cup	fresh lemon juice
2 tablespoons	pine nuts, soaked 1 hour
1–2	garlic cloves

Combine the arugula, tomatoes, onions, and salt in a large bowl. Place the parsley, olive oil, lemon juice, pine nuts, and garlic in a blender and process until smooth. Pour over the vegetables and toss gently.

Asian Spinach Salad

see photo facing page 81

yield: 1–2 servings

2 cups	baby spinach
1 cup	mung bean sprouts
¼	red bell pepper, julienned
2	raw water chestnuts, peeled and thinly sliced
1	scallion, finely chopped
1½ tablespoons	sesame oil
1½ tablespoons	fresh lemon juice
1 tablespoon	finely chopped fresh lemongrass
1 tablespoon	sesame seeds
½ teaspoon	Celtic salt
Pinch	cayenne (optional)

Combine the spinach, sprouts, bell pepper, water chestnuts, and scallion in a bowl. Place the sesame oil, lemon juice, lemongrass, sesame seeds, salt, and optional cayenne in a jar. Seal tightly and shake well. Pour over the vegetables and toss gently.

Broccoli and Cauliflower Salad

yield: 2–4 servings

4 cups	broccoli florets
2 cups	cauliflower florets
1 cup	fresh peas
1	red bell pepper, finely chopped
1	ripe tomato, diced
½	cucumber, diced
1	celery stalk, finely chopped
2	scallions, finely chopped
½ cup	cold-pressed olive oil
½ cup	fresh lemon juice
2 teaspoons	Italian seasoning
1–2	garlic cloves, minced
¼ teaspoon	Celtic salt

Combine the broccoli, cauliflower, peas, bell pepper, tomato, cucumber, celery, and scallions in a large bowl. Place the olive oil, lemon juice, Italian seasoning, garlic, and salt in a jar. Seal tightly and shake well. Pour over the vegetables and toss gently. Let marinate for 1 hour in the refrigerator before serving.

Cabbage Crunch Salad

yield: 2–4 servings

½ head	green cabbage, shredded
½ head	red cabbage, shredded
1	carrot, shredded
1 cup	walnuts, soaked 1 hour and chopped
1 cup	finely chopped fresh parsley
½ cup	finely chopped red onions
¼ cup	flax oil
¼ cup	fresh lemon juice
½ teaspoon	Celtic salt

Combine the green cabbage, red cabbage, carrot, walnuts, parsley, and onions in a large bowl. Place the flax oil, lemon juice, and salt in a jar. Seal tightly and shake well. Pour over the vegetables and toss gently.

Carrot Coriander Salad

yield: 2–3 servings

3	carrots, shredded
3 tablespoons	finely chopped shallots
2 tablespoons	finely chopped fresh parsley
3 tablespoons	fresh lemon juice
2 tablespoons	cold-pressed olive oil
1 tablespoon	ground coriander
2 teaspoons	ground cumin
1 teaspoon	turmeric
Pinch	cayenne

Combine the carrots, shallots, and parsley in a large bowl. Place the lemon juice, olive oil, coriander, cumin, turmeric, and cayenne in a jar. Seal tightly and shake well. Pour over the vegetables and toss gently.

Salads

Corn Salad

yield: 1–2 servings

2 cups	fresh corn kernels
½–1 cup	finely chopped fresh cilantro
½ cup	finely chopped red bell peppers
¼ cup	finely chopped red onions
2 tablespoons	fresh lemon juice
2 tablespoons	cold-pressed olive oil
¼ teaspoon	Celtic salt
Pinch	cayenne

Combine all the ingredients in a bowl and toss gently.

Corn and Guacamole Salad

yield: 1–2 servings

1 cup	fresh corn kernels
1	ripe avocado, cubed
1	ripe tomato, chopped
¼ cup	finely chopped red onions
3 tablespoons	fresh lime juice
2 tablespoons	finely chopped fresh cilantro
2 tablespoons	cold-pressed olive oil
2 teaspoons	raw apple cider vinegar
1–2	garlic cloves, minced
½ teaspoon	ground cumin
¼ teaspoon	Celtic salt
	Lettuce leaves
	Sprouts for garnish
	Nori sheets (optional)

Combine the corn, avocado, tomato, onions, lime juice, cilantro, olive oil, vinegar, garlic, cumin, and salt in a bowl and gently toss. Spoon over lettuce leaves and garnish with sprouts. Serve with nori sheets on the side, if using.

Salads

Cucumber Mint Salad

yield: 1–2 servings

2	cucumbers, thinly sliced
2 tablespoons	finely chopped fresh mint
2 tablespoons	cold-pressed olive oil
2 tablespoons	fresh lemon juice
1	shallot, minced
¼ teaspoon	Celtic salt

Combine all the ingredients in a bowl and toss gently.

Cucumber Red Bell Pepper Salad

yield: 2–3 servings

2	cucumbers, thinly sliced
1	red bell pepper, julienned
½ cup	finely chopped leeks
¼ cup	finely chopped fresh parsley
¼ cup	cold-pressed olive oil
¼ cup	fresh lemon juice
¼ teaspoon	Celtic salt

Combine all the ingredients in a bowl and toss gently.

Five Herb Salad

yield: 2–4 servings

6 cups	mixed salad greens
1 cup	finely chopped celery
2	scallions, finely chopped
1 tablespoon	finely chopped fresh basil
1 tablespoon	finely chopped fresh parsley
1 tablespoon	finely chopped fresh mint
¼ cup	cold-pressed olive oil
¼ cup	fresh lemon juice
1–2	garlic cloves, minced
¼ teaspoon	Celtic salt

Combine all the ingredients in a bowl and toss gently.

Golden Tomato Avocado Salad

yield: 2–4 servings

2 cups	chopped ripe yellow or orange tomatoes
1	red bell pepper, finely chopped
1	cucumber, finely chopped
1	ripe avocado, diced into ½-inch cubes
⅓ cup	fresh orange juice
2 tablespoons	finely chopped fresh basil
2 tablespoons	finely chopped fresh cilantro
2 tablespoons	cold-pressed olive oil
1	garlic clove, minced
¼ teaspoon	Celtic salt

Combine all the ingredients in a bowl and toss gently.

Greek Salad

yield: 2 servings

2	cucumbers, thinly sliced
2	ripe tomatoes, diced
½ cup	sun-dried black olives
¼ cup	finely chopped red onions
2 tablespoons	cold-pressed olive oil
1 tablespoon	raw apple cider vinegar
1 tablespoon	finely chopped fresh oregano
¼ teaspoon	Celtic salt

Combine all the ingredients in a bowl and toss gently.

Greek Mixed Green Salad

1 head	romaine lettuce, cut in bite-size pieces
2	ripe tomatoes, cut into wedges
1	cucumber, thinly sliced
1 cup	thinly sliced red radishes
10	sun-dried black olives
¼ cup	cold-pressed olive oil
3 tablespoons	fresh lemon juice
1½ teaspoons	finely chopped fresh oregano
¼ teaspoon	Celtic salt
	Freshly ground pepper

Combine all the ingredients in a bowl and toss gently.

Salads

Iraqi Tomato Salad

yield: 2–3 servings

4	ripe tomatoes, sliced
1	cucumber, diced
6	scallions, finely chopped
¼ cup	cold-pressed olive oil
3 tablespoons	finely chopped fresh parsley
2 tablespoons	finely chopped fresh mint
1½ teaspoons	ground cumin
1–2	garlic cloves, minced
¼ teaspoon	Celtic salt
	Freshly ground pepper

Combine all the ingredients in a bowl and toss gently.

Italian Salad

yield: 1–2 servings

2 cups	ripe tomatoes, diced
1	ripe avocado, cubed
½ cup	finely chopped red onions
½ cup	finely chopped fresh basil
2 tablespoons	cold-pressed olive oil
1 tablespoon	finely chopped fresh oregano
1 tablespoon	chopped sun-dried black olives
1 tablespoon	fresh lemon juice
¼ teaspoon	Celtic salt
	Lettuce leaves

Combine the tomatoes, avocado, onions, basil, olive oil, oregano, olives, lemon juice, and salt in a bowl and toss gently. Serve on a bed of lettuce leaves.

Jerusalem Artichoke Salad

2 pounds	Jerusalem artichokes, thinly sliced
1	ripe tomato, cut into wedges
½ cup	finely chopped red onions
¼ cup	flax oil
3 tablespoons	finely chopped fresh parsley
2 tablespoons	raw apple cider vinegar
1–2	garlic cloves, minced
¼ teaspoon	Celtic salt

Combine all the ingredients in a bowl and toss gently.

Jicama and Jerusalem Artichoke Salad

yield: 2–4 servings

1	jicama (about 1½ pounds), peeled and julienned
3 cups	finely chopped arugula
3	Jerusalem artichokes, thinly sliced
1	red bell pepper, finely chopped
½ bunch	watercress, stems removed
8	scallions, finely chopped
6	radishes, thinly sliced
¼ cup	cold-pressed olive oil
¼ cup	fresh lemon juice
1 teaspoon	finely chopped fresh thyme, or ½ teaspoon dried
¼ teaspoon	Celtic salt

Combine all the ingredients in a bowl and toss gently.

Salads

Kale Salad

4 cups	chopped kale leaves
2 teaspoons	Celtic salt
2 tablespoons	fresh lemon juice
¼ cup	cold-pressed olive oil
2	ripe tomatoes, diced (optional)
1	ripe avocado, diced
1 cup	clover sprouts
¼ cup	finely slivered red onions

Combine the kale and salt in a large bowl and massage the salt into the kale. Let rest for 10 minutes and massage again. Add the fresh lemon juice and massage again. Add the olive oil and massage once more. Add the optional tomatoes, avocado, sprouts, and onions and toss gently but thoroughly.

Korean Bean Sprout Salad

yield: 2–4 servings

1 pound	mung bean sprouts
2 cups	shredded carrots
1 cup	baby spinach
½ cup	finely chopped celery
¼ cup	finely chopped scallions
3 tablespoons	sesame oil
2 tablespoons	Nama Shoyu
	Freshly ground pepper
	Lettuce leaves

Combine the bean sprouts, carrots, spinach, celery, scallions, sesame oil, Nama Shoyu, and pepper to taste in a bowl. Toss gently. Serve on lettuce leaves.

Mexican Jicama Salad

yield: 2 servings

2 cups	peeled and finely chopped jicama
2	ripe tomatoes, sliced
1	red bell pepper, finely chopped
1/2 cup	finely chopped red onions
1/4 cup	cold-pressed olive oil
2 tablespoons	fresh lemon juice
1 1/2 teaspoons	finely chopped fresh oregano
1/4 teaspoon	Celtic salt

Combine all the ingredients in a bowl and toss gently.

Mexican Vegetable and Greens Salad

yield: 4–6 servings

6 cups	mixed greens
2	ripe tomatoes, cut into wedges
1	zucchini, thinly sliced
1 cup	fresh corn kernels
½ cup	finely chopped red onions
¼ cup	flax oil
2 tablespoons	fresh lemon juice
1	green chile, seeded and finely chopped (optional)
1 tablespoon	finely chopped fresh oregano
¼ teaspoon	Celtic salt

Combine all the ingredients in a bowl and toss gently.

Salads

Mixed Green Salad Portuguese Style

yield: 2–4 servings

1–2	garlic cloves
2 tablespoons	finely chopped fresh mint
½ teaspoon	Celtic salt
⅓ cup	cold-pressed olive oil
6 cups	mixed greens
½	red onion, thinly sliced and separated into rings
2 tablespoons	fresh lemon juice
	Freshly ground pepper
1	ripe tomato, cut into wedges
10	sun-dried black olives
2 tablespoons	finely chopped fresh parsley

Crush the garlic and combine it with the mint and salt in a salad bowl. Stir in the olive oil and mix well. Let marinate for 30 minutes at room temperature. Add the greens and toss lightly. Add the onion rings, lemon juice, and pepper to taste. Toss gently. Garnish with the tomato, olives, and parsley.

Photo: Lasagne, page 222

Mixed Pepper Salad

yield: 2–4 servings

1	red bell pepper, thinly sliced
1	orange bell pepper, thinly sliced
1	purple bell pepper, thinly sliced
1	yellow bell pepper, thinly sliced
1	red onion, thinly sliced into rounds
½ cup	cold-pressed olive oil
¼ cup	fresh lemon juice
¼ cup	diced sun-dried black olives
3 tablespoons	finely chopped fresh parsley
1–2	garlic cloves, minced
¼ teaspoon	Celtic salt

Combine all the ingredients in a bowl and toss gently. Let marinate in the refrigerator for 1 hour before serving.

Photo: Raw-violi, page 230

Salads

Napa Cabbage Salad Bowl

yield: 2–4 servings

1 head	napa cabbage, shredded
1 cup	mung bean sprouts
1 cup	thinly sliced red radishes
1	carrot, grated
½ cup	finely chopped scallions
½	red bell pepper, julienned
6	snow peas, julienned
6 tablespoons	flax oil
6 tablespoons	fresh lemon juice
2 tablespoons	Nama Shoyu

Combine all the ingredients in a bowl and toss gently.

Rainbow Salad

yield: 2 servings

2 cups	shredded purple cabbage
1	carrot, grated
1	cucumber, diced
6	ripe cherry tomatoes, halved
1/4 cup	finely chopped red onions
1/4 cup	cold-pressed olive oil
2 tablespoons	fresh lemon juice
1 1/2 teaspoons	whole cumin seeds
1 1/2 teaspoons	ground cumin
1/4 teaspoon	Celtic salt

Combine all the ingredients in a bowl and toss gently.

Red Cabbage with Fennel Slaw

yield: 2–4 servings

1 small head	red cabbage, finely shredded
1	fennel bulb, thinly sliced
2	carrots, grated
5	scallions, finely chopped
2	celery stalks, finely chopped
3 tablespoons	flax oil
3 tablespoons	fresh lemon juice
1 tablespoon	finely chopped fresh dill weed
½ teaspoon	Celtic salt

Combine all the ingredients in a bowl and toss gently.

Romaine Tomato Salad

yield: 2–4 servings

1 head	romaine lettuce, cut in bite-size pieces
2	ripe tomatoes, cut into wedges
1	ripe avocado, diced
1	carrot, shredded
½ cup	sliced red onions
¼ cup	cold-pressed olive oil
2 tablespoons	fresh lemon juice
1 tablespoon	finely chopped fresh basil
¼ teaspoon	Celtic salt

Combine all the ingredients in a bowl and toss gently.

Snow Pea Salad

1/2 pound	snow peas, julienned
4	raw chestnuts, thinly sliced
1	carrot, shredded
1	red bell pepper, julienned
1/4 cup	finely chopped leeks
1/4 cup	fresh lemon juice
1/4 cup	sesame oil
1 tablespoon	sesame seeds
1/4 teaspoon	Celtic salt

Combine all the ingredients in a bowl and toss gently.

Spicy Wild Rice Salad

2 cups	wild rice, soaked 3–5 days (soak until soft)
2	carrots, shredded
1	ripe avocado, diced
½ cup	finely chopped fresh cilantro
½ cup	chopped ripe tomatoes
¼ cup	finely chopped scallions
2 tablespoons	cold-pressed olive oil
2 tablespoons	fresh lemon juice
1 teaspoon	minced fresh ginger
1 teaspoon	minced fresh garlic
1 teaspoon	seeded and minced jalapeño chile
¼ teaspoon	Celtic salt

Combine all the ingredients in a bowl and toss gently.

Salads

Spinach with Cilantro Cashew Dressing

yield: 4 servings

Salad

| 8 cups | spinach |
| 1 | ripe tomato, cut into wedges |

Dressing

¼ cup	flax oil
3 tablespoons	fresh lime juice
3 tablespoons	cashews, soaked 1 hour
2 tablespoons	finely chopped fresh cilantro
1	garlic clove, minced
¼ teaspoon	Celtic salt

For the salad: Combine the spinach and tomato in a large salad bowl.

For the dressing: Combine all the ingredients in a blender and process until smooth and creamy. If too thick, add a little water. Pour the dressing over the salad and toss gently.

Spinach with Mandarin Oranges Salad

yield: 2 servings

4 cups	baby spinach
1 cup	romaine lettuce, cut in bite-size pieces
1 cup	fresh mandarin orange sections
½ cup	pine nuts
¼ cup	cold-pressed olive oil
1	scallion, finely chopped
2 tablespoons	fresh orange juice
1 tablespoon	fresh lemon juice
¼ teaspoon	Celtic salt

Combine all the ingredients in a bowl and toss gently.

Summer Salad

yield: 2 servings

4 cups	mixed greens
1	ripe avocado, diced
1	ripe tomato, finely chopped
1	carrot, shredded
½ cup	finely shredded red cabbage
½ cup	chopped sunflower sprouts
¼ cup	finely chopped red onions
10	sun-dried black olives
2 tablespoons	cold-pressed olive oil
1 tablespoon	hemp seeds
1 tablespoon	raw apple cider vinegar
¼ teaspoon	Celtic salt

Combine all the ingredients in a bowl and toss gently.

Summer Squash Salad

yield: 2–4 servings

2	yellow squash, thinly sliced
2	zucchini, thinly sliced
2	ripe tomatoes, sliced
1	red bell pepper, thinly sliced
½ cup	thinly sliced red onions
2 tablespoons	finely chopped fresh dill weed
¼ cup	flax oil
¼ cup	fresh lemon juice
1	garlic clove, minced
¼ teaspoon	Celtic salt

Combine all the ingredients in a bowl and toss gently.

Tabouli

2 cups	quinoa, sprouted
1 cup	finely chopped fresh parsley
½ cup	ripe cherry tomatoes, halved
½ cup	finely chopped fresh mint
¼ cup	finely chopped cucumber
¼ cup	cold-pressed olive oil
¼ cup	fresh lemon juice
½ teaspoon	minced fresh garlic
½ teaspoon	grated fresh ginger
¼ teaspoon	Celtic salt

Combine all the ingredients in a bowl and toss gently.

Tomato Basil Salad

yield: 2 *servings*

4	ripe tomatoes, diced
1	ripe avocado, diced
1	carrot, shredded
3	Jerusalem artichokes, thinly sliced
1	celery stalk, finely chopped
1/2 cup	finely chopped fresh basil
1/2 cup	finely chopped leeks
1/4 cup	cold-pressed olive oil
1/4 cup	fresh lemon juice
1/4 teaspoon	Celtic salt
	Lettuce leaves
	Sprouts

Combine the tomatoes, avocado, carrot, Jerusalem artichokes, celery, basil, leeks, olive oil, lemon juice, and salt in a bowl and toss gently. Serve on a bed of lettuce leaves and sprouts.

Salads

Tomato Corn Salad

yield: 2–4 servings

4	ripe Roma tomatoes, diced
2 cups	fresh corn kernels
1	red bell pepper, finely chopped
¼ cup	finely chopped red onions
¼ cup	cold-pressed olive oil
3 tablespoons	finely chopped fresh cilantro
3 tablespoons	finely chopped Italian parsley
2 tablespoons	fresh lemon juice
2 tablespoons	fresh lime juice
½	jalapeño chile, seeded and finely chopped
¼ teaspoon	Celtic salt
	Freshly ground pepper

Combine all the ingredients in a bowl and toss gently.

Tomato Cucumber Salad
with Mint

yield: 1–2 servings

1	cucumber
2	ripe tomatoes, cut into wedges
½	red onion, finely chopped
¼ cup	cold-pressed olive oil
8 large	mint leaves, cut into strips
2 tablespoons	fresh lemon juice
¼ teaspoon	Celtic salt

Cut the cucumber in half lengthwise and slice it on the diagonal into
¼-inch-thick half moons. Place in a bowl with the remaining ingredients and toss gently.

Salads

Tomatoes with
Italian Parsley Dressing

yield: 2 servings

	Lettuce leaves
	Sprouts
2–3 large	ripe tomatoes, sliced
1/2 cup	finely chopped fresh parsley
3 tablespoons	cold-pressed olive oil
2 tablespoons	finely chopped fresh basil
2 tablespoons	fresh lemon juice
2–3	garlic cloves, minced
1/4 teaspoon	Celtic salt

Arrange a bed of lettuce leaves and sprouts on a serving platter or two individual salad plates. Top with the tomatoes. Combine the parsley, olive oil, basil, lemon juice, garlic, and salt in a jar. Seal tightly and shake well. Pour over the salad and serve.

Turkish Cauliflower Salad

yield: 4 *servings*

1	cauliflower, chopped
1	red bell pepper, finely chopped
8	scallions, finely chopped
12	sun-dried black olives, pitted and diced
1/4 cup	cold-pressed olive oil
3 tablespoons	finely chopped fresh parsley
1 tablespoon	fresh lemon juice
1 tablespoon	raw apple cider vinegar
1 1/2 teaspoons	finely chopped fresh oregano

Combine all the ingredients in a bowl and toss gently.

Wild Rice Salad

yield: 2–4 servings

1½ cups	wild rice, soaked 3–5 days (soak until soft)
1	ripe tomato, diced
2	celery stalks, finely chopped
1	carrot, shredded
½ cup	finely chopped red bell peppers
¼	red onion, finely chopped
¼ cup	fresh corn kernels
¼ cup	cold-pressed olive oil
2 tablespoons	finely chopped fresh parsley
2 tablespoons	fresh lemon juice
½ teaspoon	Celtic salt

Combine all the ingredients in a bowl and toss gently.

Wild Rice and Fennel Salad

yield: 2–4 servings

1 cup	wild rice, soaked 3–5 days (soak until soft)
1	fennel bulb, julienned
2	shiitake mushrooms, thinly sliced
1	scallion, finely chopped
2 tablespoons	finely chopped fresh parsley
2 tablespoons	cold-pressed olive oil
2 tablespoons	fresh lemon juice
¼ teaspoon	Celtic salt
Pinch	cayenne

Combine all the ingredients in a bowl and toss gently.

Zucchini Salad

4 medium	zucchini, sliced into ¼-inch-thick rounds
2	ripe tomatoes, diced
½ cup	finely chopped red onions
¼ cup	cold-pressed olive oil
3 tablespoons	finely chopped fresh parsley
2 tablespoons	finely chopped fresh basil
2 tablespoons	fresh lemon juice
1–2	garlic cloves, minced
¼ teaspoon	Celtic salt

Combine all the ingredients in a bowl and toss gently.

Salad Dressings

Avocado Dressing

yield: 1 ½ cups

1	ripe avocado
¼ cup	chopped white onions
¼ cup	flax oil
2 tablespoons	fresh lime juice
¼ teaspoon	dried oregano
¼ teaspoon	Celtic salt

Combine all the ingredients in a blender and process until smooth. Thin with a little water if the dressing seems too thick.

Avocado–Basil Dressing

yield: 1 ½ cups

1	ripe avocado
¼ cup	chopped fresh basil
¼ cup	cold-pressed olive oil
3 tablespoons	fresh lemon juice
1	garlic clove, minced
¼ teaspoon	Celtic salt

Combine all the ingredients in a blender and process until smooth. Thin with a little water if the dressing seems too thick.

Avocado–Garlic Dressing

yield: 1 ½ cups

1	ripe avocado
½ cup	chopped fresh parsley
2	scallions, chopped
2 tablespoons	fresh lemon juice
1–2	garlic cloves
¼ teaspoon	Celtic salt

Combine all the ingredients in a blender and process until smooth. Thin with a little water if the dressing seems too thick.

Basil Dressing

yield: 1 ¼ cups

¾ cup	cold-pressed olive oil
½ cup	fresh lemon juice
2 tablespoons	finely chopped fresh basil
½ teaspoon	Celtic salt

Combine all the ingredients in a jar. Seal tightly and shake well.

Avocado Tomato Dressing

yield: 1 1/2 cups

1	ripe avocado
1	ripe tomato
1/2 cup	chopped red onions
1	celery stalk, chopped
2 tablespoons	chopped fresh parsley
2 tablespoons	fresh lemon juice
1/4 teaspoon	Celtic salt

Combine all the ingredients in a blender and process until smooth. Thin with a little water if the dressing seems too thick.

Cilantro Lime Dressing

yield: 1 1/2 cups

1 cup	chopped fresh cilantro
1/2 cup	flax oil
1/2 cup	fresh lime juice
1	garlic clove, minced
1/4 teaspoon	Celtic salt

Combine all the ingredients in a blender and process until smooth.

Creamy Dill Dressing

yield: 4 cups

2 cups	water
1 cup	almonds, soaked 12–48 hours
½ cup	cashews, soaked 1 hour
½ cup	chopped fresh dill weed
¼ cup	fresh lemon juice
1 teaspoon	Celtic salt
½ teaspoon	onion powder

Combine all the ingredients in a blender and process until smooth.

Creamy Cilantro Dressing

yield: 4 cups

1¾ cups	water
1 cup	almonds, soaked 12–48 hours
1 cup	chopped fresh cilantro
½ cup	cashews, soaked 1 hour
¼ cup	fresh lemon juice
1 teaspoon	Celtic salt
¼ teaspoon	garlic powder
Pinch	cayenne

Combine all the ingredients in a blender and process until smooth.

Salad Dressings

Creamy Italian Dressing

yield: 4 cups

2 cups	water
1 cup	cashews, soaked 1 hour
½ cup	almonds, soaked 12–48 hours
¼ cup	fresh lemon juice
3 tablespoons	chopped fresh basil
1 teaspoon	Italian seasoning
1 teaspoon	Celtic salt

Combine all the ingredients in a blender and process until smooth.

Creamy Garlic Onion Dressing

yield: 4 cups

2 cups	water
1 cup	almonds, soaked 12–48 hours
½ cup	cashews, soaked 1 hour
2 tablespoons	fresh lemon juice
1 teaspoon	Celtic salt
½ teaspoon	onion powder
¼ teaspoon	garlic powder

Combine all the ingredients in a blender and process until smooth.

Creamy Tomato Dressing

yield: 2 ½ cups

2	ripe tomatoes, chopped
½ cup	almonds, soaked 12–48 hours
¼ cup	pine nuts, soaked 1 hour
3 tablespoons	fresh lemon juice
2 tablespoons	finely chopped fresh marjoram, or 2 teaspoons dried
1 tablespoon	cold-pressed olive oil
½ teaspoon	Celtic salt
1–2	garlic cloves

Combine all the ingredients in a blender and process until smooth. Thin with a little water if the dressing seems too thick.

Cumin Coriander Dressing

yield: 1 cup

½ cup	cold-pressed olive oil
½ cup	fresh lemon juice
1 teaspoon	ground coriander
1 teaspoon	ground cumin
1 teaspoon	Celtic salt

Combine all the ingredients in a jar. Seal tightly and shake well.

Salad Dressings

Fiesta Dressing

yield: 1 cup

½ cup	cold-pressed olive oil
½ cup	fresh lemon juice
½ teaspoon	ground cumin
¼ teaspoon	ground coriander
¼ teaspoon	Celtic salt
⅛ teaspoon	cayenne

Combine all the ingredients in a jar. Seal tightly and shake well.

Fresh Herb Vinaigrette

yield: 1 ½ cups

1 cup	cold-pressed olive oil
½ cup	fresh lemon juice
2 tablespoons	finely chopped Italian parsley
1½ tablespoons	finely chopped chives
1 tablespoon	finely chopped fresh thyme
2 teaspoons	finely chopped fresh tarragon
¼ teaspoon	Celtic salt

Combine all the ingredients in a jar. Seal tightly and shake well.

Guacamole Dressing

yield: 1 1/2 cups

1	ripe avocado
1/2 cup	pine nuts, soaked 1 hour
2 tablespoons	raw apple cider vinegar
1 tablespoon	fresh lime juice
1/4 teaspoon	Celtic salt
Pinch	cayenne

Combine all the ingredients in a blender and process until smooth. Thin with a little water if the dressing seems too thick.

Herb Dressing

yield: 3/4 cup

1/3 cup	fresh lemon juice
1/4 cup	cold-pressed olive oil
1 tablespoon	finely chopped fresh basil
1 tablespoon	finely chopped fresh dill weed
1 tablespoon	finely chopped fresh oregano
1 teaspoon	Celtic salt
1–2	garlic cloves, minced

Combine all the ingredients in a jar. Seal tightly and shake well. Refrigerate for at least 1 hour before serving.

Italian Dressing

yield: 1 cup

2	celery stalks, chopped
1/2 cup	cold-pressed olive oil
2 tablespoons	fresh lemon juice
1 1/2 teaspoons	Italian seasoning
1/2 teaspoon	Celtic salt
1	garlic clove

Combine all the ingredients in a blender and process until smooth.

Olive Oil Dressing with Tarragon

yield: 1 cup

1/2 cup	cold-pressed olive oil
1/2 cup	fresh lemon juice
1 tablespoon	finely chopped fresh parsley
1 tablespoon	finely chopped fresh tarragon
1/4 teaspoon	Celtic salt

Combine all the ingredients in a jar. Seal tightly and shake well.

Oregano Dressing

yield: 1 ½ cups

1 cup	cold-pressed olive oil
½ cup	fresh lemon juice
1 tablespoon	finely chopped fresh oregano
1 teaspoon	Celtic salt

Combine all the ingredients in a jar. Seal tightly and shake well.

Red Pepper Curry Dressing

yield: 1 ¼ cups

1 cup	chopped red bell peppers
¼ cup	cold-pressed olive oil
2 tablespoons	fresh lemon juice
1 tablespoon	curry powder
½ teaspoon	Celtic salt

Combine all the ingredients in a blender and process until smooth.

Salad Dressings

Rosemary Vinaigrette

yield: 1 1/2 cups

1 cup	cold-pressed olive oil
6 tablespoons	raw apple cider vinegar
2 tablespoons	dry mustard
1/2 teaspoon	finely chopped fresh rosemary
1/2 teaspoon	Celtic salt

Combine all the ingredients in a jar. Seal tightly and shake well.

Sesame Dressing

yield: 1 1/4 cups

1/2 cup	raw tahini
1/2 cup	cold-pressed olive oil
1/4 cup	fresh lemon juice
1/4 cup	finely chopped fresh parsley
2	garlic cloves, minced
1/4 teaspoon	Celtic salt
Pinch	cayenne

Combine all the ingredients in a jar. Seal tightly and shake well.

Spicy Curry Dressing

yield: 1 cup

½ cup	flax oil
½ cup	fresh lemon juice
2 tablespoons	grated fresh ginger
1 tablespoon	ground cumin
2 teaspoons	curry powder
1 teaspoon	ground cinnamon
1 teaspoon	ground coriander
½ teaspoon	ground cardamom
½ teaspoon	Celtic salt
Pinch	cayenne

Combine all the ingredients in a jar. Seal tightly and shake well.

Salad Dressings

Tomato Basil Dressing

yield: 1 cup

1 large	ripe tomato, chopped
½ cup	sun-dried tomatoes, soaked 2 hours
¼ cup	soak water from sun-dried tomatoes
¼ cup	finely chopped fresh basil
2 tablespoons	cold-pressed olive oil
1 tablespoon	raw apple cider vinegar
1	garlic clove, minced
¼ teaspoon	Celtic salt

Combine all the ingredients in a blender and process until smooth.

Tomato Herb Dressing

yield: 1 1/2 cups

1 cup	ripe tomatoes, chopped
1/2 cup	cold-pressed olive oil
2 tablespoons	chopped fresh basil
2 tablespoons	fresh lemon juice
1 tablespoon	Italian seasoning
1/2 teaspoon	Celtic salt
	Freshly ground pepper

Combine all the ingredients in a blender and process until smooth and creamy.

Zucchini Herb Dressing

yield: 1 1/2 cups

1 cup	chopped zucchini
3 tablespoons	fresh lemon juice
2 tablespoons	cold-pressed olive oil
1 tablespoon	finely chopped fresh basil
1 tablespoon	finely chopped chives
1 1/2 teaspoons	finely chopped fresh thyme
1 teaspoon	Celtic salt
Pinch	cayenne

Combine all the ingredients in a blender and process until smooth and creamy.

Sea Vegetables

Sea vegetables are marine algae and are among the most nutritious plants on Earth. They provide our bodies with vitamins, minerals, protein, carbohydrates, fats, and trace nutrients. Since our blood contains all of the elements found in seawater, there is no better way to provide the body with a full spectrum of nutrients than by consuming sea vegetables. Sea vegetables are available at natural food stores, Chinese and Japanese markets, and other specialty stores. There are many different kinds of sea vegetables, and they come in an array of sizes, shapes, and colors. Enjoy sea vegetables daily and have fun creating your own delicacies with them.

Arame Salad

yield: 1–2 servings

½ cup	arame, soaked 15–30 minutes
2 tablespoons	finely chopped chives
2 tablespoons	finely chopped fresh herbs (such as basil, dill weed, cilantro, or parsley)
1 tablespoon	cold-pressed olive oil
1 tablespoon	fresh lemon juice
1	garlic clove, minced
¼ teaspoon	Celtic salt

Combine all the ingredients in a bowl and toss gently.

Arame Carrot Salad

yield: 1–2 servings

½ cup	arame, soaked 15–30 minutes
1	carrot, shredded
1	celery stalk, finely chopped
2	scallions, finely chopped
1 tablespoon	sesame seeds
1 tablespoon	flax oil
1 tablespoon	fresh lemon juice
½ teaspoon	minced fresh ginger
¼ teaspoon	Celtic salt

Combine all the ingredients in a bowl and toss gently.

Arame Veggie Salad

yield: 2–3 servings

1 cup	mung bean sprouts
½ cup	arame, soaked 15 minutes
1	carrot, shredded
½	red bell pepper, thinly sliced
10	snow peas, julienned
3	scallions, finely chopped
¼ cup	fresh lemon juice
2 tablespoons	cold-pressed olive oil
¼ teaspoon	Celtic salt

Combine all the ingredients in a bowl and toss gently.

Arame Zucchini Salad

yield: 2–3 servings

1	zucchini, julienned
1 cup	finely chopped red bell peppers
½ cup	arame, soaked 15 minutes
2	celery stalks, finely chopped
¼ cup	finely chopped leeks
¼ cup	fresh lemon juice
2 tablespoons	cold-pressed olive oil
1 tablespoon	finely chopped fresh basil
¼ teaspoon	Celtic salt

Combine all the ingredients in a bowl and toss gently.

Sea Vegetables

Asian Wakame Salad

yield: 1–2 servings

1 cup	mung bean sprouts
1 cup	julienned snow peas
½ cup	wakame, soaked 15 minutes
½	red bell pepper, julienned
2	Jerusalem artichokes, thinly sliced
2	scallions, finely chopped
¼ cup	fresh lemon juice
2 tablespoons	flax oil
1 tablespoon	finely chopped fresh cilantro
1 teaspoon	grated fresh ginger
¼ teaspoon	Celtic salt
Pinch	cayenne

Combine all the ingredients in a bowl and toss gently.

Avocado Wakame Salad

yield: 1–2 servings

1	ripe avocado, diced
1	cucumber, thinly sliced
½ cup	wakame, soaked 15 minutes
2	scallions, finely chopped
¼ cup	fresh lemon juice
2 tablespoons	finely chopped fresh basil
2 tablespoons	cold-pressed olive oil
¼ teaspoon	Celtic salt

Combine all the ingredients in a bowl and toss gently.

Avocado Dulse Salad

yield: 1–2 servings

Serve this salad on a bed of lettuce or your favorite sprouts, or roll or wrap it in a sheet of nori.

1	ripe avocado, mashed
1	ripe tomato, finely diced
½ cup	dulse, rinsed and chopped
¼ cup	finely chopped red bell peppers
¼ cup	finely chopped red onions
1	celery stalk, finely chopped
1 tablespoon	cold-pressed olive oil
1 tablespoon	fresh lemon juice

Combine all the ingredients in a bowl and mix well.

Carrot Sea Vegetable Salad

yield: 2–3 servings

Serve this salad with clover, sunflower, or buckwheat sprouts.

3	carrots, shredded
1	red bell pepper, thinly sliced
1 cup	dulse, rinsed and chopped
2 tablespoons	finely chopped leeks
2 tablespoons	cold-pressed olive oil
2 tablespoons	fresh lemon juice
Pinch	cayenne

Combine all the ingredients in a bowl and mix well.

Sea Vegetables

Corn Salad with Wakame

yield: 2–3 servings

2 cups	fresh corn kernels
1 cup	peeled and diced jicama
½ cup	finely chopped red bell peppers
¼ cup	finely chopped leeks
¼ cup	wakame, soaked 15 minutes
¼ cup	fresh lemon juice
2 tablespoons	finely chopped fresh parsley
2 tablespoons	flax oil
1 tablespoon	sesame seeds
¼ teaspoon	Celtic salt

Combine all the ingredients in a bowl and toss gently.

Dulse Salad

yield: 4–6 servings

3	carrots, grated
1	apple, thinly sliced
1 cup	chopped clover sprouts
½	ripe avocado, diced
½ cup	flax oil
¼ cup	fresh lemon juice
¼ cup	Nama Shoyu
3 ounces	dulse, finely chopped

Combine all the ingredients in a bowl and toss gently.

Dulse Cucumber Salad

yield: 2–3 servings

1	cucumber, thinly sliced
1 cup	fresh corn kernels
1 cup	dulse, rinsed and chopped
½ cup	finely chopped red bell peppers
½ cup	finely chopped fresh parsley
2	scallions, finely chopped
2 tablespoons	cold-pressed olive oil
2 tablespoons	fresh lemon juice

Combine all the ingredients in a bowl and toss gently.

Dulse and Walla Walla Onions

yield: 1–2 servings

Spoon this salad over lettuce leaves and serve it with green sprouts.

1	cucumber, thinly sliced
1 small	Walla Walla onion, finely chopped
½ cup	dulse, rinsed and chopped
2 tablespoons	finely chopped fresh parsley
1 tablespoon	cold-pressed olive oil
1 tablespoon	fresh lemon juice

Combine all the ingredients in a bowl and toss gently.

Sea Vegetables

Hijiki Carrot Salad

yield: 1–2 servings

2 cups	shredded carrots
½ cup	hijiki, soaked 15–30 minutes
1	celery stalk, finely chopped
3 tablespoons	sesame oil
3 tablespoons	fresh lemon juice
1–2 teaspoons	grated fresh ginger
¼ teaspoon	Celtic salt

Combine all the ingredients in a bowl and toss gently.

Mediterranean Wakame Salad

yield: 2–3 servings

½ cup	wakame, soaked 15 minutes
½ cup	chopped sun-dried black olives
2	celery stalks, finely chopped
4	red radishes, thinly sliced
4	shiitake mushrooms, thinly sliced
2	scallions, finely chopped
3 tablespoons	fresh lemon juice
2 tablespoons	cold-pressed olive oil
1	garlic clove, minced
Pinch	cayenne

Combine all the ingredients in a bowl and toss gently.

Hijiki Corn Salad

yield: 2–3 servings

2 cups	fresh corn kernels
½ cup	hijiki, soaked 15–30 minutes
½ cup	finely chopped red bell peppers
¼ cup	finely chopped red onions
2 tablespoons	cold-pressed olive oil
2 tablespoons	fresh lemon juice
¼ teaspoon	Celtic salt

Combine all the ingredients in a bowl and toss gently.

Sea Vegetables

Sea Vegetable Salad

yield: 2–3 servings

1	ripe tomato, finely chopped
½ cup	chopped sun-dried black olives
½	red bell pepper, thinly sliced
¼ cup	dulse, soaked 5 minutes
¼ cup	wakame, soaked 15 minutes
2	celery stalks, finely chopped
2	scallions, finely chopped
2 tablespoons	cold-pressed olive oil
2 tablespoons	fresh lemon juice
1 tablespoon	sesame seeds
¼ teaspoon	Celtic salt

Combine all the ingredients in a bowl and toss gently.

Main Dishes

A Holiday Dinner

A totally raw meal for any special occasion.

MENU (SERVES 8—10)

Cranberry Sauce
Holiday Patties
Mashed "Potatoes" with Gravy (page 228)
Pumpkin Bread (page 80)
Salad (prepare your favorite green salad)
Tastes Like Pumpkin Pie (page 301)

Cranberry Sauce

yield: 8–10 servings

2 cups	fresh cranberries
1	orange
1	apple
4	pitted dates, soaked 30 minutes
	Water as needed

Combine all the ingredients in a blender and process until smooth. Add just enough water to facilitate blending.

Holiday Patties

yield: 8–10 servings

Tastes like stuffing!

1 cup	almonds, soaked 12–48 hours
1 cup	pecans, soaked 1 hour
1 cup	pumpkin seeds, soaked 6 hours
1 cup	finely chopped fresh parsley
1 cup	finely chopped leeks
¼ cup	fresh lemon juice
3 tablespoons	golden flaxseeds, ground superfine
2 tablespoons	poultry seasoning
1½ teaspoons	Celtic salt
½ teaspoon	kelp powder
	Clover sprouts

Combine the almonds, pecans, and pumpkin seeds in a food processor fitted with the S blade and process into a fine meal. Transfer to a bowl and stir in the parsley, leeks, lemon juice, flaxseeds, poultry seasoning, salt, and kelp powder. Mix well.

Form into 2-inch round patties and place on a dehydrator tray with a Teflex sheet. Dehydrate at 105 degrees for 2 hours. Turn the patties over, remove the Teflex sheet, and continue dehydrating for 3 hours longer. The patties should be crisp on the outside and warm and moist on the inside. Serve warm on a bed of clover sprouts.

Main Dishes

Burritos

Tortillas (makes seven or eight 6-inch tortillas)

1 cup	flaxseeds, soaked in 1 cup water for 4–6 hours (see note)
1/2	ripe avocado
1/2 cup	water as needed
1/2 teaspoon	Celtic salt

Combine all the ingredients in a blender, adding just enough water to facilitate blending. Process until smooth. Spread 1/3 cup of the batter evenly on Teflex sheets, forming a circle about 1/8 inch thick and 6 inches in diameter. The thinner the batter, the less time it will take to dehydrate the tortillas (and the better they will taste). Dehydrate at 105 degrees for 2–3 hours. Flip the tortillas over and remove the Teflex sheets. Continue to dehydrate for 2 hours longer or until the tortillas are soft and flexible. Remove the tortillas from the dehydrator before they become crisp. For the best results, dehydrate the tortillas the day before you plan to use them.

Burritos (continued)

Note: Alternatively, instead of soaking, the flaxseeds may be ground in a coffee grinder or blender. Add 1 cup of water to the blender when processing the tortilla mixture.

To make a perfect circle, I use an old plastic storage container lid and cut out the center to use as a template.

Mock Refried Bean Pâté

2 cups	almonds, soaked 12–48 hours
1 cup	sun-dried tomatoes, soaked 2–4 hours
1 tablespoon	Mexican seasoning
2 teaspoons	fresh lemon juice (optional)
1½ teaspoons	raw red miso (optional)
1 teaspoon	Celtic salt

Combine all the ingredients in a food processor fitted with the S blade and process until smooth and creamy. If the mixture seems too thick, add a little water to achieve the desired consistency.

(recipe continues next page)

Main Dishes

Burritos (continued)

Guacamole

1	ripe tomato, chopped
¼ cup	finely chopped fresh cilantro
¼ cup	minced white onions
1 tablespoon	fresh lime juice
1 small	jalapeño chile, seeded and finely chopped
3	ripe avocados
	Celtic salt

Combine the tomatoes, cilantro, onions, lime juice, and chile in a bowl. Mash the avocados and stir into the tomato mixture. Season with salt to taste.

Fresh Tomato Salsa

3 large	ripe tomatoes, diced
1 small	red onion, finely chopped
½	red bell pepper, finely chopped
3–4 tablespoons	finely chopped fresh parsley or cilantro
½	jalapeño chile, seeded and minced
2 tablespoons	fresh lime juice
1 small	garlic clove, minced

Combine all the ingredients in a bowl and mix well.

To assemble the burrito: Spread each tortilla with some of the pâté and top with the guacamole and salsa. Fold the tortilla gently.

Cabbage Burritos

yield: 6–8 servings

1 large head   red cabbage
Pâté (your choice of the pâtés on pages 110–122)
Green sprouts
Ripe tomatoes, sliced or chopped
Ripe avocados, sliced or chopped
Onions, sliced or chopped
Carrots, grated

Cut the bottom of the cabbage so it is flat and carefully peel off the cabbage leaves. If you have difficulty, try cutting off a bit more of the bottom of the cabbage. Stuff the leaves with the pâté, sprouts, tomatoes, avocados, onions, and carrots.

Enchiladas

yield: 6–8 servings

6–8   nori sheets, cut in half lengthwise
(extra-thin sheets work best)
Cheeze Filling from Chiles Rellenos (page 216)
Mole Sauce from Chiles Rellenos (page 217)

Place a sheet of nori on a cutting board and spoon some of the cheeze filling on the narrow end of the sheet. Roll the nori sheet and seal the end by rubbing a little water on the nori. Place on a serving dish and spoon the mole sauce over the nori roll. Let rest for 15–30 minutes before serving.

Main Dishes

Carrot Zucchini Nut Patties

yield: 20 patties

2 cups	pecans, soaked 1 hour
2 cups	chopped broccoli
5	carrots
2	zucchini
1 cup	sun-dried tomatoes, soaked 4–6 hours
½ cup	fresh cilantro
½ cup	fresh parsley
¾ cup	golden flaxseeds, ground
¼ cup	fresh lemon juice
1 tablespoon	Italian seasoning
2	garlic cloves, minced
2 teaspoons	dried marjoram
1½ teaspoons	Celtic salt
½ teaspoon	ground cinnamon
¼ teaspoon	ground allspice
¼ teaspoon	cayenne

Process the pecans, broccoli, carrots, zucchini, sun-dried tomatoes, cilantro, and parsley separately (each ingredient by itself) in a food processor fitted with the S blade until very finely chopped. Transfer each ingredient to a large bowl after it is processed. Stir in the ground flaxseeds, lemon juice, Italian seasoning, garlic, marjoram, salt, cinnamon, allspice, and cayenne and mix using your hands. Continue working the mixture until it no longer sticks to your hands but is still very moist. Form into small patties, about 3 inches in diameter and ¼ inch thick. Place on a dehydrator tray and dehydrate at 105 degrees for 6–8 hours or until the desired dryness is achieved. The patties should be crispy on the outside and a little moist on the inside.

Chili

yield: 4–6 servings

3 cups	fresh tomato juice
½ cup	lentils, sprouted
1	carrot, grated
¼ cup	finely chopped celery
¼ cup	fresh corn kernels
¼ cup	fresh lemon juice
¼ cup	finely chopped red bell pepper
¼ cup	finely chopped white onions
¼ cup	finely chopped zucchini
2 teaspoons	chili powder
1–2	garlic cloves, minced
1 teaspoon	Celtic salt
¼ teaspoon	ground cumin
Pinch	cayenne

Combine all the ingredients in a large bowl. Let marinate several hours in the refrigerator before serving.

Main Dishes

Chiles Rellenos

see photo facing page 80   *yield: 6 servings*

Chiles

6	Anaheim chiles

$\mathcal{C}$ut each chile in half lengthwise and scoop out the seeds. Set aside.

Cheeze Filling

1 cup	almonds, soaked 12–48 hours
½ cup	sunflower seeds, soaked 6–8 hours
¼ cup	macadamia nuts, soaked 1 hour
¼ cup	pine nuts, soaked 1 hour
1 cup	chopped red bell peppers
2 tablespoons	nutritional yeast
2 tablespoons	fresh lemon juice
¼ teaspoon	Celtic salt
¼–½ cup	coconut water or water as needed

$\mathcal{C}$ombine the almonds, sunflower seeds, macadamia nuts, and pine nuts in a food processor fitted with the S blade and process into a fine meal. Add the red bell pepper, nutritional yeast, lemon juice, and salt and process until smooth and creamy. Add just enough coconut water to facilitate processing.

Chiles Rellenos (continued)

Mole Sauce

1	red bell pepper
1 small	ripe tomato
1–2	pitted dates
1 tablespoon	raw carob powder
2 teaspoons	fresh lemon juice
¼ teaspoon	Celtic salt
¼ teaspoon	chili powder
Pinch	cayenne
	Water as needed

Combine all the ingredients in a blender and process until smooth and creamy. Use just enough water to facilitate blending.

To assemble: Stuff the chile halves with the cheeze filling and pour the mole sauce over them.

Note: Chiles Rellenos may be served cold or warm. To warm them, place the stuffed chiles in a dehydrator at 105 degrees for 3–4 hours.

Main Dishes

Falafel

Falafel

1½ cups	garbanzo beans, soaked 8 hours and sprouted
1 cup	sunflower seeds, soaked 6–8 hours and rinsed
1	red onion, finely chopped
¼ cup	finely chopped fresh parsley
¼ cup	cold-pressed olive oil
2 tablespoons	fresh lemon juice
1–2	garlic cloves, minced
1 teaspoon	Celtic salt
1 teaspoon	ground coriander
1 teaspoon	ground cumin
¼ teaspoon	cayenne

Process the garbanzo beans and sunflower seeds through a Champion Juicer with the solid plate, or in a food processor fitted with the S blade. Stir in the remaining ingredients and mix well. Form into small patties, about 2 inches wide and ½ inch thick, and place on a dehydrator tray. Dehydrate at 105 degrees for 16–18 hours or until the desired dryness is achieved.

Falafel (continued)

Tahini Sauce

1/2 cup	raw tahini
1/4 cup	finely chopped fresh parsley
1 tablespoon	fresh lemon juice
1 small	garlic clove, minced
1/4 teaspoon	Celtic salt
	Water as needed

Combine all the ingredients in a blender or a food processor fitted with the S blade. Process until smooth to make a thin, creamy sauce.

Wrappers and Condiments

Large lettuce or cabbage leaves, or Pita Bread (page 79)
Ripe tomatoes, sliced
Cucumber
Ripe avocado

To serve falafel: Place one or two falafel on a lettuce or cabbage leaf or in a Pita Bread. Drizzle with some of the sauce and add tomato, cucumber, and avocado to taste. Roll the wrapper around the falafel and vegetables and serve.

Main Dishes

Italian Casserole

Casserole

2 cups	almonds, soaked 12–48 hours
1 cup	sunflower seeds, soaked 6–8 hours and rinsed
3	celery stalks
2	carrots
¼ cup	minced onions
1 teaspoon	Celtic salt
1–2	garlic cloves, minced
	Italian seasoning

*P*rocess the almonds, sunflower seeds, celery, and carrots through a Champion Juicer with the solid plate, or in a food processor fitted with the S blade. Transfer to a bowl and stir in the onions, salt, garlic, and Italian seasoning to taste. Mix well. Spread the mixture in an 8 x 8-inch glass dish and pat it down lightly.

Italian Casserole (continued)

Topping

3 large	ripe Roma tomatoes, or 2 large ripe tomatoes
¾ cup	sun-dried tomatoes, soaked 4–6 hours
½ cup	finely chopped fresh basil
½ cup	finely chopped Italian parsley
1 tablespoon	cold-pressed olive oil
2 teaspoons	fresh lemon juice
1	garlic clove, minced
½ teaspoon	Celtic salt
½ teaspoon	dried oregano
½ teaspoon	dried rosemary
½ teaspoon	dried stevia leaves

Cut the fresh tomatoes in half, scoop out and discard the seeds, and chop finely. Transfer to a medium bowl. Combine the sun-dried tomatoes, basil, parsley, oil, lemon juice, garlic, salt, oregano, rosemary, and stevia in a blender and process until smooth. Add to the fresh tomatoes and mix well.

To assemble casserole: Spoon the topping evenly over the casserole. Refrigerate for 1 hour before serving.

Main Dishes

Lasagne

see photo facing page 160

yield: 6–8 servings

This is one of my favorite recipes. My Italian heritage loves this dish.

Zucchini Noodles

4	zucchini
	Celtic salt

Thinly slice the zucchini lengthwise into long, flat, ⅛-inch strips. (It will be easier to slice thin, even strips if you first cut the zucchini in half lengthwise.) Place the slices on a clean towel and sprinkle lightly with Celtic salt. Let rest for 15–20 minutes. Dry the zucchini with a paper towel to remove the salt and moisture. Arrange half of the zucchini strips in an 8 x 12-inch glass dish. Reserve the remaining half.

Macadamia Nut Ricotta Cheeze

1½ cups	macadamia nuts
¼ cup	pine nuts, soaked 1 hour
2 tablespoons	nutritional yeast
1 teaspoon	Celtic salt
2 tablespoons	cold-pressed olive oil
6–8 tablespoons	water as needed

Lasagne (continued)

Combine the macadamia nuts, pine nuts, nutritional yeast, and salt in a food processor fitted with the S blade and process into a fine meal. Gradually add the olive oil and just enough water to make a smooth, thick sauce. Spread the cheeze over the zucchini noodles in the glass dish.

Marinated Mushrooms

3	portobello mushrooms, thinly sliced
1/2 cup	finely chopped fresh basil
3	scallions, finely chopped
1/4 cup	cold-pressed olive oil
2 tablespoons	fresh lemon juice
1 teaspoon	dried stevia leaves
1 teaspoon	Celtic salt

Combine all the ingredients in a medium bowl and toss gently. Marinate in the refrigerator for 6–8 hours or overnight. Drain the liquid from the mushrooms and layer them over the cheeze. Top with the reserved zucchini strips.

(recipe continues next page)

Main Dishes

Lasagne (continued)

Sun-Dried Tomato Marinara

6	ripe Roma tomatoes, or 4 large ripe tomatoes
1½ cups	sun-dried tomatoes, soaked 4–6 hours
1 cup	finely chopped fresh basil
1 cup	finely chopped Italian parsley
2 tablespoons	cold-pressed olive oil
1 tablespoon	fresh lemon juice
1 teaspoon	Celtic salt
1 teaspoon	dried oregano
1 teaspoon	dried rosemary
1 teaspoon	dried stevia leaves
1	garlic clove, minced

Cut the fresh tomatoes in half, scoop out and discard the seeds, and chop finely. Transfer to a medium bowl. Combine the sun-dried tomatoes, basil, parsley, olive oil, lemon juice, salt, oregano, rosemary, stevia, and garlic in a blender and process until smooth. Stir into the fresh tomatoes and mix well.

To assemble the lasagne: Spoon the marinara over the top layer of zucchini noodles. Refrigerate for 1 hour before serving.

Greek Patties

Serve these patties in a large lettuce leaf or Pita Bread (page 79) with sliced tomatoes, sprouts, cucumber, and avocado.

2½ cups	almonds, soaked 12–48 hours
2 cups	finely chopped fresh cilantro
½ cup	finely chopped white onions
½ cup	cold-pressed olive oil
½ cup	raw tahini
½ cup	fresh lemon juice
2 tablespoons	finely chopped fresh parsley
1½ teaspoons	ground cumin
1–2	garlic cloves, minced
1 teaspoon	Celtic salt
¼ teaspoon	curry powder

*P*rocess the almonds through a Champion Juicer with the solid plate, or in a food processor fitted with the S blade. Transfer to a bowl and add the remaining ingredients. Mix well. Form into patties about 2 inches wide and ½ inch thick, and place on a dehydrator tray. Dehydrate for 16–18 hours at 105 degrees or until the desired dryness is achieved.

Manicotti

yield: 6–8 servings

Nori Noodles

6–8	nori sheets (extra-thin sheets work best)

Cut the nori sheets in half lengthwise and reserve.

Ricotta Cheeze

1½ cups	macadamia nuts, soaked 1 hour
¼ cup	pine nuts, soaked 1 hour
2 tablespoons	nutritional yeast
1 teaspoon	Celtic salt
2 tablespoons	cold-pressed olive oil
6–8 tablespoons	water as needed

Combine the macadamia nuts, pine nuts, nutritional yeast, and salt in a food processor fitted with the S blade and process into a fine meal. Gradually add the olive oil and just enough water to make a smooth, thick sauce.

Manicotti (continued)

Tomato Marinara

4 large	ripe tomatoes
1 cup	fresh basil
1 cup	Italian parsley
1½ cups	sun-dried tomatoes, soaked 4–6 hours (reserve soak water)
2 tablespoons	cold-pressed olive oil
1–2	garlic cloves, minced
1 teaspoon	Celtic salt
1 teaspoon	Italian seasoning
1 teaspoon	dried stevia leaves

Cut the fresh tomatoes in half, scoop out and discard the seeds, and chop finely. Transfer to a medium bowl. Place the basil and parsley in a food processor fitted with the S blade and process until finely chopped. Add the sun-dried tomatoes and a small amount of their soak water, just enough to facilitate blending, and process into a thick sauce. Add ⅔ cup of the chopped fresh tomatoes along with the olive oil, garlic, salt, Italian seasoning, and stevia leaves and process into a moderately thick sauce. Pour into the bowl with the remaining fresh tomatoes and mix well.

To assemble the dish: Place a half-sheet of nori on a cutting board and spoon some of the cheeze on the narrow end of the sheet. Roll the nori sheet and seal the end by rubbing it with a little water. Fill the remaining nori sheets in a similar fashion until all of the cheeze is used. Place on a serving dish and spoon the marinara over the top. Let rest for 15–30 minutes before serving.

Main Dishes

Mashed "Potatoes" with Mushroom Gravy

yield: 4–6 servings

"Potatoes"

4 cups	chopped cauliflower
1/2 cup	pine nuts, soaked 1 hour
1/2 cup	cashews, soaked 1 hour
3 tablespoons	cold-pressed olive oil
1 1/2 tablespoons	Italian seasoning
1 1/2 teaspoons	garlic, minced
1/2 teaspoon	Celtic salt
	Freshly ground pepper

Combine all the ingredients in a food processor fitted with the S blade and process until smooth and creamy. If too thick, add a little water to achieve the desired consistency.

Mashed "Potatoes" with Mushroom Gravy
(continued)

Mushroom Gravy

1/2 cup	almonds, soaked 12–48 hours and blanched (see page 34)
1/2 cup	water
1 1/2 cups	whole shiitake mushrooms
1/2 cup	finely chopped shiitake mushrooms
1/4 teaspoon	garlic granules, or 1 garlic clove, minced
1/2 teaspoon	Celtic salt

Combine the almonds and water in a blender and process until smooth and creamy. Transfer to a bowl and set aside. Place the whole shiitake mushrooms in the blender and process until smooth and creamy, adding a little water as needed to facilitate blending and achieve the desired consistency. Stir into the blended almonds. Stir in the chopped shiitake mushrooms, garlic, and salt and mix well. Serve the gravy over the Mashed "Potatoes" or on the side.

Main Dishes

Raw-violi

see photo facing page 161

yield: 6–8 servings

*Raw-violi can be made with either eggplant or watermelon daikon
(which are also called watermelon radish). Both are delicious.*

Eggplant Raw-violi

2	eggplants, sliced into paper-thin rounds
1 teaspoon	Celtic salt

Fill a large bowl with warm water. Add the salt and stir to dissolve.
Add the eggplant slices and let soak for 2 hours. Drain well.

Daikon Raw-violi

2	watermelon daikon

Slice into paper-thin rounds.

Raw-violi (continued)

Filling

1½ cups	macadamia nuts, soaked 1 hour
½ cup	pine nuts, soaked 1 hour
2 tablespoons	cold-pressed olive oil
1½ tablespoons	Italian seasoning
1½ tablespoons	fresh lemon juice
1 teaspoon	Celtic salt
1–2	garlic cloves, minced
6–8 tablespoons	water as needed
1–2 tablespoons	minced fresh basil

Combine the macadamia nuts and pine nuts in a food processor fitted with the S blade and process into a fine meal. Add the olive oil, Italian seasoning, lemon juice, salt, and garlic. Process into a very thick sauce or paste, adding just enough water to facilitate blending. Transfer to a small bowl and stir in the basil. Mix well.

To assemble the eggplant raw-violi: Place 1 tablespoon of the filling on half of each eggplant round and fold into a half moon. Place on a dehydrator tray and dehydrate for 3–4 hours at 105 degrees. Serve warm with Marinara Sauce (recipe follows) or your favorite sauce.

recipe continues next page

Main Dishes

Raw-violi (continued)

To assemble the daikon raw-violi: Place 1 tablespoon of the filling on half of each daikon round and fold into a half moon. Serve immediately with Marinara Sauce (recipe follows) or your favorite sauce. (Do not dehydrate.)

Marinara Sauce

6	ripe Roma tomatoes
1/3 cup	sun-dried tomatoes, soaked 4 hours (reserve soak water)
7	black mission figs, soaked 4 hours (reserve soak water)
3	scallions, chopped
1/4 cup	fresh parsley
1 tablespoon	fresh lemon juice
1	garlic clove, minced
1/2 teaspoon	dried oregano
1/2 teaspoon	Celtic salt

Combine all the ingredients in a food processor fitted with the S blade, or in a blender, and process until smooth. If the sauce is too thick, add a little of the tomato or fig soak water.

Mushroom Burgers

yield: 6–8 servings

see photo facing page 280

1 cup	almonds, soaked 12–48 hours
1 cup	walnuts, soaked 8 hours
1 cup	sunflower seeds, soaked 6–8 hours and rinsed
1	red onion, finely chopped
1½ cups	finely chopped portobello mushrooms
1 cup	finely chopped red bell peppers
½ cup	finely chopped celery
½ cup	finely chopped fresh parsley
¼ cup	cold-pressed olive oil
3 tablespoons	golden flaxseeds, ground superfine
2 teaspoons	Celtic Salt
1½ teaspoons	minced fresh ginger
1 teaspoon	dried tarragon
1–2	garlic cloves, minced

Process the almonds, walnuts, and sunflower seeds through a Champion Juicer with the solid plate, or in a food processor fitted with the S blade. (If you use a food processor, add a little water with the nuts to make a smooth paste.) Transfer to a large bowl and add the remaining ingredients. Mix well.

Form into patties about 4 inches wide and ½ inch thick. Place on a dehydrator tray with a Teflex sheet. Dehydrate at 105 degrees for 6 hours. Remove the Teflex sheet and continue dehydrating for 8–10 hours longer or until the desired dryness is achieved. The burgers should be crispy on the outside and slightly moist inside.

Main Dishes

Spanish Rice

yield: 4 servings

2 cups	wild rice, soaked 3–5 days (soak until soft)
1/2 cup	finely chopped fresh cilantro
4	scallions, finely chopped
2	celery stalks, finely chopped
1	ripe tomato, finely chopped
1/2	red bell pepper, finely chopped
2 tablespoons	cold-pressed olive oil
2 tablespoons	fresh lemon juice
1 tablespoon	jalapeño chile, seeded and finely chopped
1 teaspoon	Celtic salt
1/8–1/4 teaspoon	chili powder

Combine all the ingredients in a large bowl and mix well.

Stuffed Tomatoes

see photo facing page 81

yield: 4 servings

4 extra-large	ripe tomatoes
	Spicy Wild Rice Salad (page 167)
	or Wild Rice Salad (page 178)

Scoop out the center of each tomato with a spoon. Stuff with the wild rice salad of your choice.

Stuffed Bell Peppers

yield: 6 servings

2 cups	almonds, soaked 12–48 hours
1 cup	sunflower seeds, soaked 4 hours
1	carrot
¾ cup	finely chopped fresh parsley
½ cup	finely chopped red onions
3	celery stalks, finely chopped
2 tablespoons	fresh lemon juice
1 teaspoon	Celtic salt
Pinch	cayenne
3 large	red bell peppers
	Grated carrots for garnish
	Mint leaves for garnish

For the filling: Process the almonds, sunflower seeds, and carrot through a Champion Juicer with the solid plate, or in a food processor fitted with the S blade. If using a food processor, add about ¼ cup water to help make a smooth paste. Transfer to a bowl and stir in the parsley, onions, celery, lemon juice, salt, and cayenne. Mix well.

To stuff the peppers: Cut off the tops of the red bell peppers and remove the seeds and ribs. Stuff with the filling and garnish with grated carrots and mint leaves.

Variation: Place the stuffed peppers on a dehydrator tray and dehydrate for 3–4 hours at 105 degrees. Serve warm.

Main Dishes

Spaghetti with Marinara Sauce

yield: 4–6 servings

Vegetable Spaghetti (choose one)

3 large	sweet potatoes OR
3 large	yams OR
4 large	zucchini

Process the vegetable of your choice through a fine vegetable shredder or other kitchen tool (such as a spiral vegetable slicer) that will produce the look and feel of angel hair pasta.

Marinara Sauce

8	ripe Roma tomatoes, seeded and chopped
½ cup	sun-dried tomatoes, soaked 2 hours (reserve soak water)
¼ cup	chopped fresh parsley
2	scallions, chopped
3 tablespoons	cold-pressed olive oil
2 tablespoons	Italian seasoning
2 teaspoons	fresh lemon juice
2	garlic cloves, minced
1 teaspoon	Celtic salt
1 teaspoon	dried stevia leaves

Combine all the ingredients in a blender and process until smooth and creamy. If necessary, add a little of the sun-dried tomato soak water to achieve the desired consistency.

To assemble: Pour the sauce over the vegetable spaghetti and serve.

Thai Patties

yield: 20 patties

2 cups	almonds, soaked 12–48 hours
1/2 cup	sunflower seeds, soaked 4 hours
2	carrots
1	zucchini
1/2 cup	dulse flakes or finely chopped dulse
1/2 cup	finely chopped fresh parsley
1 tablespoon	ground cumin
1 tablespoon	turmeric
1 teaspoon	Celtic salt

Process the almonds, sunflower seeds, carrots, and zucchini through a Champion Juicer with the solid plate. Transfer to a bowl and stir in the remaining ingredients. Mix well. Form into round patties, about 1½ inches in diameter and ¼ inch thick. Place on a dehydrator tray and dehydrate at 105 degrees for 4–6 hours or until the desired dryness is achieved.

Main Dishes

Pad Thai with Mock Peanut Sauce

yield: 2–4 servings

Pad Thai

2 cups	young coconut pulp, julienned
1½ tablespoons	minced fresh chives
1½ tablespoons	hulled white sesame seeds, soaked 1 hour
1 tablespoon	minced fresh lemongrass
1 tablespoon	sesame oil
1½ teaspoons	Nama Shoyu
½ teaspoon	Celtic salt
Pinch	cayenne
½ cup	chopped mung beans for garnish
½ cup	finely chopped cashews for garnish

Combine the coconut pulp, chives, sesame seeds, lemongrass, sesame oil, Nama Shoyu, salt, and cayenne in a bowl and mix well. Dehydrate for 1–2 hours at 105 degrees or until warm. Garnish with the mung beans and cashews. Serve warm.

recipe continues next page

Pad Thai (continued)

Mock Peanut Sauce

1/2 cup	sesame oil or cold-pressed olive oil
1/4 cup	date paste (dates and water blended)
2 tablespoons	finely chopped fresh ginger
2 tablespoons	light miso
1 tablespoon	raw apple cider vinegar, or 2 tablespoons fresh lemon juice
1 tablespoon	Nama Shoyu
1	garlic clove, minced (optional)
Pinch	cayenne

Combine all the ingredients in a blender and process until smooth and creamy. Serve with the pad thai.

Thai Noodles

yield: 2–4 servings

2 cups	young coconut pulp, julienned
1 1/2 tablespoons	minced fresh chives
1 1/2 tablespoons	sesame seeds
1 tablespoon	minced fresh lemongrass
1 tablespoon	sesame oil
1 1/2 teaspoons	Nama Shoyu
1/2 teaspoon	Celtic salt
Pinch	cayenne

Combine all the ingredients in a bowl and mix well. Dehydrate for 1–2 hours at 105 degrees or until warm.

Main Dishes

Veggie Burgers

yield: 6–8 servings

Serve these burgers in a large lettuce leaf with a slice of tomato, onion, and avocado.

1 cup	almonds, soaked 12–48 hours
1 cup	sunflower seeds, soaked 4 hours and rinsed
1	red onion
1	zucchini
1 small	beet
1	red bell pepper
2	carrots, finely grated
2	celery stalks, finely chopped
1/4 cup	finely chopped fresh parsley
2 tablespoons	flaxseeds, ground superfine
2 tablespoons	fresh lemon juice
1 1/2 teaspoons	Celtic salt

Process the almonds, sunflower seeds, onion, zucchini, beet, and bell pepper through a Champion Juicer using the solid plate, or in a food processor fitted with the S blade. Transfer to a bowl and add the remaining ingredients. Mix well. Form into patties about 4 inches wide and 1/2 inch thick. Place on a dehydrator tray with a Teflex sheet. Dehydrate for 4 hours at 105 degrees. Turn the burgers over and remove the Teflex sheet. Continue dehydrating for 4–6 hours longer or until the desired dryness is achieved. The burgers should be crispy on the outside and a little moist on the inside.

Desserts

Cakes

If your food processor is small, you might have difficulty processing a full cake recipe in it. In this case, simply divide the recipe in half and process each half separately; then combine the two portions in a bowl to finish the recipe. Many of my cake recipes call for dates. I prefer honey dates or medjool dates for making cakes, as they are moist, meaty, and soft.

Autumn Anniversary Cake

yield: 25–35 servings

Cake

3 cups	almonds, soaked 12–48 hours
3 cups	pecans, soaked 1 hour
3 cups	raisins
3 cups	pitted dates
4 teaspoons	vanilla extract

Combine the almonds and pecans in a food processor fitted with the S blade and process into a fine meal. Gradually add the raisins, dates, and vanilla. Continue processing until the mixture is smooth and forms a ball. Divide into two equal parts (for two layers) and form into the desired shape.

Icing

1 cup	cashews, soaked 1 hour
1/2 cup	macadamia nuts, soaked 1 hour
1/2 cup	pitted dates
1/4 cup	pine nuts, soaked 1 hour
1/2 cup	water
3 tablespoons	raw almond butter
2 teaspoons	vanilla extract

Autumn Anniversary Cake (continued)

Combine all the ingredients in a food processor fitted with the S blade and process until smooth and creamy. Add a little water if needed to achieve the desired consistency.

To assemble the cake: Place the bottom layer of cake on a serving platter and ice the top of it. Place the second layer of cake on top of the first layer, and ice the top and sides. Refrigerate for at least 30 minutes before serving.

Decoration

Ripe Fuji persimmons, thinly sliced
Raisins

To decorate: Arrange the persimmon slices in a small circle over the icing. Fill the center of the circle with raisins.

Desserts

Apricot Torte

Torte

2 cups	pecans, soaked 1 hour
2 cups	raisins
1 teaspoon	vanilla extract

Place the pecans in a food processor fitted with the S blade and process into a fine meal. Slowly add the raisins and vanilla and process until the mixture forms a small ball. Transfer to a cake plate or round serving platter and form into a 6-inch round cake approximately 1 inch high.

Icing

½ cup	dried apricots, soaked 4 hours
¼ cup	cashews, soaked 1 hour
1 teaspoon	vanilla extract

Process the apricots in a food processor fitted with the S blade, or in a blender. Gradually add the cashews and vanilla. Add a little water if needed to achieve the desired consistency. The icing should be smooth, thick, and creamy. Spread over the torte.

Banana and Fig Torte

yield: 8–10 servings

Torte

1 cup	pecans, soaked 1 hour
1 cup	pine nuts, soaked 1 hour
2 cups	raisins
1 cup	black mission figs
4	dried bananas
2 teaspoons	vanilla extract

Combine the pecans and pine nuts in a food processor fitted with the S blade and process into a fine meal. Gradually add the raisins, figs, bananas, and vanilla and continue processing until the mixture forms a ball. Divide into two equal parts (for two layers) and form into the desired shape.

Icing

2 cups	cashews, soaked 1 hour
¼ cup	pure maple syrup, or ½ cup pitted dates
3 tablespoons	raw carob powder (add more for a darker, extra-rich icing)

Combine all the ingredients in a blender and process until smooth and creamy. Add a little water if needed to achieve the desired consistency. The icing should be thick and creamy.

To assemble the cake: Place the bottom layer of cake on a serving platter and ice the top of it. Place the second layer of cake on top of the first layer, and ice the top and sides.

Desserts

Carrot Cake

This cake can only be made in a Champion Juicer or a Green Power Juicer.

Cake

3 cups	chopped carrots
½ cup	almonds, soaked 12–48 hours
½ cup	hazelnuts
¼ cup	pine nuts, soaked 1 hour
2	apples, shredded
½ cup	walnuts, soaked 1 hour and chopped
½ cup	raisins
¼ cup	shredded dried coconut
1 tablespoon	psyllium powder
1 teaspoon	vanilla extract
½ teaspoon	Celtic salt
¼ teaspoon	ground cinnamon

Process the carrots, almonds, hazelnuts, and pine nuts through a Champion Juicer with the solid plate. Transfer to a bowl and stir in the remaining ingredients. Mix well. Press firmly into an 8 x 8-inch glass dish.

Carrot Cake (continued)

Icing

¾ cup	cashews, soaked 1 hour
¼ cup	pitted dates
¼ cup	pine nuts, soak 1 hour
¼ cup	water
2 tablespoons	fresh lemon juice
1 teaspoon	vanilla extract

Combine all the ingredients in a blender and process until smooth, creamy, and thick.

To assemble the cake: Spread the icing over the cake. Refrigerate for 1–2 hours before serving.

Desserts

Cheesecake with Fruit Topping

see photo facing page 281

see photo facing page 281

yield: 12 servings

Cheesecake

4 cups	almonds, soaked 12–48 hours and blanched (see page 34)
¼ cup	fresh lemon juice
2 cups	pitted dates
1 teaspoon	almond extract
1 teaspoon	vanilla extract
¼ teaspoon	Celtic salt

Line a pie plate with cheesecloth and set aside. Combine the almonds and lemon juice in a blender and process until smooth and creamy. Add a little water if needed to achieve the desired consistency. Pour into a juice bag and squeeze out the liquid until the pulp is a moist pâté. Transfer to a food processor fitted with the S blade. Add the remaining ingredients and process until smooth and well combined. Spread into the prepared pie plate and pat until firm. Turn the pie plate over onto a flat dish and carefully remove the cheesecloth.

Cheesecake with Fruit Topping (continued)

Topping

12	dried apricots, soaked 2–4 hours
6	pitted dates, soaked 1 hour (reserve soak water)

Combine the apricots and dates in a blender and process until smooth and creamy. Add a little of the date soak water as needed to achieve the desired consistency. Spread over the top of the cheesecake.

Fruit Decoration

Thinly sliced fruit or berries (such as kiwifruit, peaches, pears, bananas, strawberries, or blueberries)

Decorate the cheesecake with the thinly sliced fruit or berries of your choice. Refrigerate the cheesecake for 2–3 hours before serving.

Cosmic Strawberry Banana Cake

yield: 12–16 servings

This cake is processed in two batches to make it easier for most food processors to handle. Decorate the cake with edible fresh flowers or place thinly sliced strawberries over the entire top of the cake for a beautiful finish.

Cake

1½ cups	almonds, soaked 12–48 hours
1½ cups	pecans, soaked 1 hour
3 cups	pitted dates
¼ cup	raw carob powder
2 teaspoons	vanilla extract

Combine ¾ cup of the almonds and ¾ cup of the pecans in a food processor fitted with the S blade and process into a fine meal. Gradually add 1½ cups of the dates, 2 tablespoons of the carob powder, and 1 teaspoon of the vanilla. Continue processing until the mixture forms a smooth ball. Transfer to a plate and shape into a rectangle (this will be the first layer). Process the remaining ingredients in the same fashion. Transfer to a plate and form into a rectangle (this will be the second layer). Place both layers in the refrigerator while you make the icing.

Cosmic Strawberry Banana Cake
(continued)

Strawberry Icing

1 cup	cashews, soaked 1 hour
1 cup	strawberries
¼ cup	pitted dates
¼ cup	pine nuts, soaked 1 hour
1 teaspoon	vanilla extract

Combine all the ingredients in a blender and process until smooth, creamy, and thick. Chill in the refrigerator for 1 hour.

Banana Filling

1	ripe banana, sliced

To assemble: Ice the first layer of the cake and decorate the top with a layer of the sliced bananas. Place the second layer of the cake on top of the bananas and ice with the remaining icing.

Decadent Carob Cake

yield: 8–10 servings

Cake

2 cups	walnuts, soaked 1 hour
2 cups	pitted medjool dates
¼ cup	raw carob powder
¼ cup	raw almond butter
2 teaspoons	vanilla extract

Place the walnuts in a food processor fitted with the S blade and process into a fine meal. Gradually add the dates, carob powder, almond butter, and vanilla and continue processing until the mixture forms a small ball. Divide into two equal parts. Place each part on a plate and form into the desired shape.

Filling

1 tablespoon	pure maple syrup or raw honey
1 tablespoon	raw carob powder
1 tablespoon	raw almond butter

Combine all the ingredients in a blender or food processor fitted with the S blade and process until smooth and creamy. Add a little water if needed to achieve the desired consistency. The filling should be thick and creamy. Spread evenly over the top of the bottom layer. Place the second layer over the filling.

Decadent Carob Cake
(continued)

Icing

1	ripe avocado
5	pitted medjool dates
1/3 cup	pine nuts, soaked 30 minutes
1 teaspoon	vanilla extract

Combine the avocado, dates, nuts, and vanilla in a blender or a food processor fitted with the S blade and process until smooth and creamy. Add a little water if needed to achieve the desired consistency. The icing should be thick and creamy. Spread evenly over the cake with a spatula or knife. Refrigerate for 2–3 hours before serving.

Decoration

Edible fresh flowers (optional)

To decorate: Decorate the iced cake with edible fresh flowers, if desired.

Desserts

Decadent Carob Strawberry Torte

yield: 15–20 servings

This recipe was developed by Colleen Holland.

Torte

4 cups	pecans, soaked 1 hour
2 cups	pitted medjool dates
¼ cup	raw almond butter
¼ cup	raw carob powder
2 teaspoons	vanilla extract

Place the pecans in a food processor fitted with the S blade and process into a fine meal. Gradually add the dates, almond butter, carob powder, and vanilla and continue processing until the mixture is smooth and forms a ball. Divide into two equal parts and set aside.

Carob Icing

1 cup	pure maple syrup
¾ cup	raw carob powder
¾ cup	raw almond butter
1 teaspoon	pure vanilla extract

Decadent Carob Strawberry Torte
(continued)

Combine all the ingredients in a food processor fitted with the S blade and process until smooth and creamy.

Filling

1 cup	sliced strawberries

Topping Decoration

6 large	strawberries
¼ cup	Carob Icing
¼ cup	finely chopped pecans

To assemble: Place one part of the torte on a round cake plate and mold it into a round layer. Spread half of the Carob Icing over the top and arrange the filling of sliced strawberries over it. Mold the other part of the torte into the same size and shape and place it on top of the sliced strawberries (a spatula may be helpful when transferring the top layer). Reserve ¼ cup of the Carob Icing and spread the remaining icing over the top layer of the torte. For the topping decoration, dip the 6 strawberries in the reserved ¼ cup of Carob Icing and roll them in the chopped pecans. Place them in a circle on top of the cake. Refrigerate the cake for 2–3 hours before serving.

recipe continues next page

Decadent Carob Strawberry Torte
(continued)

Strawberry Coulis

1 cup	strawberries
3 tablespoons	pure maple syrup

Combine the strawberries and maple syrup in a blender and process until smooth. Pour into a plastic squeeze bottle.

Cashew Crème

1 cup	cashews, soaked 1 hour
½ cup	pitted medjool dates, soaked in water for 30 minutes
1½ teaspoons	vanilla extract

Combine all the ingredients in a food processor fitted with the S blade and process until smooth and creamy. Add a little water if needed to achieve the desired consistency.

Garnish

Fresh mint leaves (optional)

To serve: Draw a pattern with the Strawberry Coulis on individual dessert plates. Place one slice of the torte on top of the coulis and put a dollop of the Cashew Crème beside it. Garnish each serving with a fresh mint leaf, if desired.

Cherry Fantasy Cake

yield: 10–15 servings

Cake

2 cups	Brazil nuts, soaked 6 hours
1 cup	pitted honey dates or medjool dates, at room temperature
1 cup	raisins, at room temperature
1/4 cup	raw carob powder
1 teaspoon	vanilla extract

Place the Brazil nuts in a food processor fitted with the S blade and process into a fine meal. Gradually add the dates, raisins, carob powder, and vanilla and continue processing until the mixture is smooth and forms a ball. Divide into two equal parts (for two layers) and form into the desired shape.

Icing

2 cups	cashews or macadamia nuts, soaked 1 hour
1 cup	dried Bing cherries, soaked 1 hour
1/2 cup	pitted dates, soaked 15 minutes

Combine all the ingredients in a food processor fitted with the S blade and process until smooth and creamy. Add a little water if needed to achieve the desired consistency.

To assemble: Place the bottom layer of cake on a serving platter and ice the top. Place the second layer of cake on top of the first layer, and ice the top and sides. Refrigerate for at least 30 minutes before serving.

Desserts

Heavenly Peach Cake

First Layer

2 cups	almonds, soaked 12–48 hours and dehydrated 8 hours at 105 degrees
2 cups	raisins

Place the almonds in a food processor fitted with the S blade and process into a fine meal. Gradually add the raisins and continue processing until the mixture forms a ball. Place on a cake plate and form into the desired shape.

Second Layer

2 cups	pecans, soaked 1 hour
2 cups	pitted dates
1 teaspoon	coconut or vanilla extract

Place the pecans in a food processor fitted with the S blade and process into a fine meal. Gradually add the dates and coconut extract and continue processing until the mixture forms a ball. Form into the same shape as the first layer.

Filling

2	ripe peaches
1 cup	pine nuts, soaked 30 minutes

Heavenly Peach Cake
(continued)

Combine the peaches and pine nuts in a food processor fitted with the S blade, or in a blender, and process until smooth and creamy. Add a little water if needed to achieve the desired consistency. Refrigerate for 1 hour. Spread evenly over the first layer and place the second layer on top.

Topping

1 cup	pitted dates
1 cup	pine nuts, soaked 30 minutes
1 teaspoon	vanilla extract

Combine all the ingredients in a food processor fitted with the S blade, or in a blender, and process until smooth and creamy. Refrigerate for 1 hour. Spread evenly over the top of the cake (do not ice the sides of the cake).

Decoration for the Sides

¼ cup	finely chopped pecans

To decorate the sides: Press the finely chopped pecans evenly on all sides of the cake. Refrigerate for 2–3 hours before serving.

Desserts

Pineapple Surprise

yield: 10–12 servings

Cake

2 cups	pecans, soaked 1 hour
2 cups	pitted dates
½ cup	raw carob powder
2 teaspoons	vanilla extract

Place the pecans in a food processor fitted with the S blade and process into a fine meal. Gradually add the dates, carob powder, and vanilla and continue processing until the mixture is smooth and forms a ball. Divide the cake into two equal parts (for two layers) and place each part on a plate. Shape each part into a round layer and place in the refrigerator for about 30 minutes to set.

Icing

2 cups	cashews, soaked 1 hour
1 cup	fresh or frozen pineapple

Combine the cashews and pineapple in a food processor fitted with the S blade, or in a blender, and process until smooth and creamy. Add a little water if needed to achieve the desired consistency. The icing should be thick and creamy.

Pineapple Surprise (continued)

Filling

1	ripe banana, thinly sliced
¼ teaspoon	ground cinnamon

Decoration

Shredded dried coconut
Edible fresh flowers
Pineapple slices

To assemble: Ice the first layer of the cake and top it with a layer of the thinly sliced bananas. Sprinkle the bananas lightly with cinnamon. Place the second layer of the cake on top of the bananas and ice the whole cake. Sprinkle with coconut and decorate with edible fresh flowers and slices of pineapple.

Desserts

Strawberry Almond Cake

yield: 10–12 servings

First Layer

2 cups	almonds, soaked 12–48 hours
2 cups	pitted honey dates or medjool dates
2 teaspoons	vanilla extract

*P*lace the almonds in a food processor fitted with the S blade and process into a fine meal. Gradually add the dates and vanilla and continue processing until the mixture is smooth and forms a ball. Form into your favorite shape (round, square, rectangle, or heart).

Second Layer

2 cups	almonds, soaked 12–48 hours
2 cups	raisins
2 teaspoons	vanilla extract

*P*lace the almonds in a food processor fitted with the S blade and process into a fine meal. Gradually add the raisins and vanilla and continue processing until the mixture is smooth and forms a ball. Form into the same shape as the first layer.

Strawberry Almond Cake *(continued)*

Icing

2 cups	cashews, soaked 1 hour
1 cup	strawberries
¼ cup	pitted dates, soaked 1 hour
1 teaspoon	vanilla extract

Combine all the icing ingredients in a food processor fitted with the S blade, or in a blender, and process until smooth and creamy.

Filling

½ cup	thinly sliced strawberries

Decoration

Fresh flowers

To assemble: Ice the first layer of cake and layer the sliced strawberries on top. Place the second layer of cake over the sliced strawberries and ice the top and sides of the cake with the remaining icing. Decorate the top of the cake with fresh flowers.

Yuletide Log

Cake

2 cups	walnuts, soaked 1 hour
2 cups	pitted dates
¼ cup	raw carob powder
½ teaspoon	peppermint extract

Place the walnuts in a food processor fitted with the S blade and process into a fine meal. Gradually add the dates, carob powder, and peppermint extract and continue processing until the mixture is smooth and forms a ball. Roll between two pieces of waxed paper to form a 15 x 7 x ¼-inch rectangle. Refrigerate for 2 hours.

Filling

1 cup	cashews, soaked 1 hour
½ cup	pine nuts, soaked 1 hour
5 large	pitted dates, soaked 1 hour
2 tablespoons	water
¼ teaspoon	vanilla extract

Combine all the ingredients in a food processor fitted with the S blade, or in a blender, and process until smooth and creamy. The filling should be thick and creamy. Add additional water if needed to achieve the desired consistency.

Yuletide Log *(continued)*

Icing

¼ *cup*	raw carob powder
2 *tablespoons*	raw honey
1 *tablespoon*	raw almond butter
1 *teaspoon*	vanilla extract

Combine all the ingredients in a food processor fitted with the S blade, or in a blender, and process until smooth and creamy. Add a little water if needed to achieve the desired consistency. The icing should be thick and creamy.

Decoration

Fresh flowers and greenery

To assemble: Spread the filling evenly over the top of the cake. Carefully roll the cake into a round log. Spread the icing on the top of the log. Decorate with fresh flowers and greenery.

Desserts

Candies

Carob Fudge

yield: 64 (1-inch) pieces

1½ cups	pecans, soaked 30 minutes
1 cup	pine nuts, soaked 30 minutes
1 cup	pitted honey dates or medjool dates
1 cup	walnuts, soaked 1 hour and chopped
6 tablespoons	raw carob powder
1 teaspoon	vanilla extract

Process the pecans, pine nuts, and dates through a Champion Juicer with the solid plate, or in a food processor fitted with the S blade. Stir in the walnuts, carob powder, and vanilla and mix well. Spread the mixture evenly in a rectangular 8 x 8-inch glass dish. Score the fudge into squares. Cover and store in the freezer. Serve cold.

Divine Truffles

2 cups	pecans, soaked 2–4 hours
2 cups	pitted dates
1 tablespoon	raw carob powder
1 teaspoon	vanilla extract
	Shredded dried coconut

*P*lace the pecans in a food processor fitted with the S blade and process into a fine meal. Gradually add the dates, carob powder, and vanilla and continue processing until the mixture forms a ball. Form into ¾-inch balls and roll them in shredded coconut until evenly coated all over.

Variations: To vary the flavor, replace the vanilla with a different extract (such as peppermint, coconut, or orange). To make the truffles richer and smoother, add ¼ cup pine nuts that have been soaked for 1 hour.

Desserts

Heavenly Truffles

yield: 30 truffles

1 cup	cashews, soaked 1 hour
½ cup	macadamia nuts, soaked 1 hour
¼ cup	pine nuts, soaked 1 hour
¾ cup	pitted dates
¾ cup	raisins
2–3 tablespoons	raw carob powder
2 teaspoons	vanilla extract
	Shredded dried coconut, carob powder, or ground nuts

Combine the cashews, macadamia nuts, and pine nuts in a food processor fitted with the S blade and process into a fine meal. Gradually add the dates, raisins, carob powder, and vanilla and process until the mixture forms a ball. Form into ¾-inch balls and roll them in shredded coconut, carob powder, or ground nuts until evenly coated all over.

Lemon Truffles

2 cups	pecans, soaked 1 hour
2 cups	pitted medjool dates
2 tablespoons	raw almond butter
1 teaspoon	vanilla extract
1 teaspoon	lemon extract
	Shredded dried coconut

Place the pecans in a food processor fitted with the S blade and process into a fine meal. Gradually add the dates, almond butter, and vanilla and lemon extracts and process until the mixture forms a ball. Form into ¾-inch balls and roll them in shredded coconut until evenly coated all over.

Desserts

Orange Truffles

2 cups	Brazil nuts, soaked 6 hours
1 cup	raisins
¾ cup	black mission figs, soaked 1 hour
3–4 tablespoons	raw carob powder
2 teaspoons	vanilla extract
2 teaspoons	orange extract
	Shredded dried coconut

*P*lace the Brazil nuts in a food processor with the S blade and process into a fine meal. Gradually add the raisins, figs, carob powder, and vanilla and orange extracts and process until the mixture forms a ball. Form into ¾-inch balls and roll them in shredded coconut until evenly coated all over.

Cookies

Apple Cinnamon Cookies

yield: about 35 cookies

2 cups	sunflower seeds, soaked 6–8 hours and rinsed
2	apples, chopped
½ cup	pitted dates
1 cup	walnuts, soaked 2 hours and chopped
2 tablespoons	golden flaxseeds, ground
1 teaspoon	Celtic salt
1 teaspoon	ground cinnamon
1 teaspoon	vanilla extract

Process the sunflower seeds, apples, and dates through a Champion Juicer with the solid plate, or in a food processor fitted with the S blade. Stir in the remaining ingredients and mix well. Form into cookies about 1½ inches in diameter and about ½ inch thick and place on a dehydrator tray. Dehydrate at 105 degrees for 8–10 hours.

Desserts

Apple Energy Bars

yield: 16–20 bars

2	apples, coarsely chopped
1 cup	sesame seeds, soaked 6–8 hours
2/3 cup	pumpkin seeds, soaked 6–8 hours
2/3 cup	sunflower seeds, soaked 6–8 hours
2 tablespoons	flaxseeds, ground
2 tablespoons	water
1 teaspoon	ground cinnamon
1 teaspoon	vanilla extract
1/4 teaspoon	Celtic salt

Place the apples in a food processor fitted with the S blade and process until finely grated. Transfer to a bowl and stir in the remaining ingredients. Mix well. Spread the mixture evenly, about 1/4 inch thick, on a dehydrator tray with a Teflex sheet. Score the bars before dehydrating. Dehydrate at 105 degrees for 6 hours. Remove the Teflex sheet and continue dehydrating for 10–12 hours or until very crispy. Store in a glass container in the refrigerator.

Apricot Cookies

yield: 20 cookies

2 cups	almonds, soaked 12–48 hours
½ cup	pine nuts, soaked 1 hour
2 cups	dried Turkish apricots, soaked 1 hour (reserve soak water)
¼ cup	golden flaxseeds, ground superfine
1 teaspoon	ground cinnamon
1 teaspoon	vanilla extract
½ teaspoon	ground cardamom
½ teaspoon	Celtic salt

Combine the almonds and pine nuts in a food processor fitted with the S blade and process into a fine meal. Gradually add the apricots and ¼ cup of their soak water. Process until thoroughly blended. Transfer to a bowl and stir in the flaxseeds, cinnamon, vanilla, cardamom, and salt. Spoon the dough onto a dehydrator tray with a Teflex sheet and form into cookies about 1½ inches in diameter and about ½ inch thick. Dehydrate at 105 degrees for 6 hours. Turn the cookies over and remove the Teflex sheet. Continue dehydrating for 12–16 hours or until the desired crispness is achieved.

Desserts

Apricot Coconut Cookies

yield: 24 cookies

2 cups	pecans, soaked 1 hour
2 cups	dried Turkish apricots
1 teaspoon	vanilla extract
½ cup	shredded dried coconut

Place the pecans in a food processor fitted with the S blade and process into a fine meal. Gradually add the apricots and vanilla and process until the mixture is thoroughly blended and forms a ball. Form the dough into cookies about 1½ inches in diameter and ¼ inch thick and roll them in the shredded coconut until they are completely covered. Store the cookies in a glass container in the refrigerator.

Apricot Hemp Cookies

yield: 25 cookies

1 cup	sunflower seeds, soaked 6–8 hours and rinsed
1 cup	dried Turkish apricots, soaked 1 hour
1	ripe banana
½ cup	water
1 cup	chopped walnuts
½ cup	hemp seeds
½ cup	raisins
2 teaspoons	vanilla extract
1 teaspoon	ground cardamom
1 teaspoon	ground cinnamon

Combine the sunflower seeds, apricots, banana, and water in a blender and process until smooth, thick, and creamy. Transfer to a bowl and stir in the remaining ingredients. Mix well. Form into cookies about 2 inches in diameter and ½ inch thick and place on a dehydrator tray. Dehydrate at 105 degrees for 8–10 hours or until the desired crispness is achieved.

Desserts

Asian Almond Cookies

2 cups	almonds, soaked 12–48 hours and blanched (see page 34)
1	apple, peeled
1 cup	pitted dates, soaked 15 minutes in warm water
1 teaspoon	vanilla extract
1/2 teaspoon	almond extract
15	almonds, soaked 12–48 hours, blanched and halved, for garnish

Process the 2 cups of almonds, apple, and dates through a Champion Juicer with the solid plate, or in a food processor fitted with the S blade. Transfer to a bowl and stir in the remaining ingredients. Mix well. Spoon a heaping tablespoon of dough onto a dehydrator tray and shape into cookies about 2 inches in diameter and 1/4 inch thick. Press an almond half into the middle of each cookie. Dehydrate at 105 degrees for 12–16 hours or until the desired crispness is achieved.

Note: If a food processor is used for making the cookies, add a little water (up to 1/4 cup) as needed to help smooth the mixture.

Living in the Raw   276

Carrot Raisin Cookies

yield: about 27 cookies

2 cups	pecans, soaked 1 hour
3	carrots
2	apples
1 cup	golden flaxseeds, ground superfine
¾ cup	raisins
½ cup	walnuts, soaked 1 hour and chopped
1 teaspoon	Celtic salt
1 teaspoon	ground cinnamon
1 teaspoon	vanilla extract

*P*lace the pecans in a food processor fitted with the S blade and process into a fine meal. Transfer to a bowl. Place the carrots in a food processor fitted with the S blade and chop superfine. Add to the pecans. Place the apples in a food processor with the S blade and chop superfine. Add to the pecans and carrots. Stir in the remaining ingredients and mix well. Form into cookies about 2½ inches in diameter and ½ inch thick and place on a dehydrator tray. Dehydrate at 105 degrees for 14–16 hours or until the desired crispness is achieved.

Desserts

Cherry Fudge Brownies

yield: 25–30 brownies

Brownies

2 cups	pecans, soaked 1 hour
½ cup	pine nuts, soaked 1 hour
½ cup	pitted dates
¼ cup	raw carob powder
2	Fuji apples, grated
1 cup	walnuts, soaked 1 hour and chopped
2 tablespoons	golden flaxseeds, ground superfine
1 teaspoon	Celtic salt
1 teaspoon	vanilla extract

Combine the pecans and pine nuts in a food processor fitted with the S blade and process into a fine meal. Gradually add the dates and carob powder and continue processing until well blended. Transfer to a bowl and stir in the apples, walnuts, flaxseeds, salt, and vanilla. Mix well. Form into 1½-inch squares, about ½ inch thick. Place on a dehydrator tray and dehydrate at 105 degrees for 12–14 hours or until the desired dryness is achieved. The brownies should be crispy on the outside and somewhat soft on the inside, but not completely dried out. Cool before icing.

Cherry Fudge Brownies *(continued)*

Note: The apples may be finely chopped (separately) in a food processor fitted with the S blade, or grated using the grating attachment, and then combined with the remaining ingredients.

Icing

½ cup	dried Bing cherries, soaked 1 hour
¼ cup	pitted dates, soaked 10 minutes (reserve soak water)
¼ cup	raw carob powder
1 teaspoon	vanilla extract

Combine the Bing cherries, dates, carob powder, and vanilla in a food processor fitted with the S blade and process until smooth and creamy. Add some of the date soak water as needed to achieve the desired consistency. Chill in the refrigerator before icing the brownies. Ice the brownies after they are completely cool.

Desserts

Fig Coconut Cookies

yield: 24 cookies

2 cups	pecans, soaked 1 hour
2½ cups	dried black mission figs, stems removed
2 teaspoons	vanilla extract
1 cup	shredded dried coconut

Place the pecans in a food processor fitted with the S blade and process into a fine meal. Gradually add the black mission figs and vanilla. Process until thoroughly blended. Form into cookies about 1½ inches in diameter and ¼ inch thick. Carefully roll in the shredded coconut, completely covering each cookie. Store in a glass container in the refrigerator.

Photos: Mushroom Burgers, page 233

Hazelnut Coconut Cookies

yield: 24 cookies

1 cup	hazelnuts, soaked 6 hours
1 cup	pitted dates
1 teaspoon	vanilla extract
½ teaspoon	ground cinnamon
½ teaspoon	ground nutmeg
¼ teaspoon	Celtic salt
1 cup	shredded dried coconut

Place the hazelnuts in a food processor fitted with the S blade and process into a fine meal. Gradually add the dates, vanilla, cinnamon, nutmeg, and salt and process until thoroughly blended. Form the dough into cookies about 1½ inches in diameter and ¼ inch thick. Roll in the shredded coconut, completely covering each cookie. Store in a glass container in the refrigerator.

Top Photo: Tomato Soup, page 130, Apple Zucchini Bread (left), page 69, Mexican Flax Crackers (right), page 92
Bottom Photo: Cheesecake with Fruit Topping, page 248

Desserts

Lemon Bars

yield: 16 (2 x 2-inch) bars

Bars

1 cup	almonds, soaked 12–48 hours
1 cup	Brazil nuts, soaked 6 hours
2 cups	raisins
1 tablespoon	lemon zest
1 tablespoon	fresh lemon juice
1 teaspoon	vanilla extract
¼ teaspoon	Celtic salt

Combine the almonds and Brazil nuts in a food processor fitted with the S blade and process into a fine meal. Gradually add the raisins and the lemon zest, lemon juice, vanilla, and salt and process until the mixture is thoroughly blended and forms a ball. Press the dough into an 8 x 8-inch glass dish.

Icing

1 cup	pitted dates
¼ cup	fresh lemon juice
1 tablespoon	lemon zest

Combine all the ingredients in a blender and process until smooth and creamy. Ice the top of the bars and refrigerate for 1–2 hours before serving.

Lemon Coconut Bars

yield: 16 (2 x 2-inch) bars

2 cups	pecans, soaked 1 hour
2 cups	pitted dates
1 tablespoon	lemon zest
1 tablespoon	fresh lemon juice
1 teaspoon	vanilla extract
1 cup	shredded dried coconut

Place the pecans in a food processor fitted with the S blade and process into a fine meal. Gradually add the dates and the lemon zest, lemon juice, and vanilla and process until the dough is completely blended and forms a ball. Press the dough into an 8 x 8-inch glass dish. Sprinkle the top with the shredded coconut and pat lightly.

Desserts

Oatmeal Cookies

yield: 24–30 cookies

2 cups	oat groats, soaked 12 hours
¾ cup	water
¼–½ cup	pitted dates
2	apples, grated
½ cup	raisins
1½ teaspoons	ground cinnamon
1 teaspoon	vanilla extract
½ teaspoon	Celtic salt

Combine the oat groats, water, and dates in a food processor fitted with the S blade (or in a high-speed, heavy-duty blender) and process until thoroughly blended. Transfer to a bowl and stir in the apples, raisins, cinnamon, vanilla, and salt. Mix well. Spoon the dough onto a dehydrator tray with a Teflex sheet and form into small cookies about 2 inches in diameter and ½ inch thick. Dehydrate at 105 degrees for 6 hours. Turn the cookies over and remove the Teflex sheet. Continue dehydrating for 12–14 hours or until desired crispness is achieved. The cookies should be crispy on the outside and moist on the inside.

Persimmon Cookies

yield: 40 cookies

2 cups	sunflower seeds, soaked 6–8 hours and rinsed
2 large	very ripe persimmons
¼–½ cup	water
½ cup	pitted honey dates
1 teaspoon	vanilla extract
1 teaspoon	ground cinnamon
½ teaspoon	Celtic salt
1 cup	raisins
1 cup	walnuts, soaked 1 hour and chopped

Combine the sunflower seeds, persimmons, and ¼ cup of the water in a blender and process until smooth and thick. Add more water if needed to facilitate blending. Add the dates, vanilla, cinnamon, and salt and continue processing until well blended. Transfer to a bowl and stir in the raisins and walnuts. Mix well. Spoon the dough on a dehydrator tray with a Teflex sheet and form into small cookies 1½ inches in diameter and ½ inch thick. Dehydrate at 105 degrees for 4–6 hours. Turn the cookies over and remove the Teflex sheet. Continue dehydrating for 4–6 hours or until the desired crispness is achieved.

Desserts

Thumbprint Cookies

Cookies

1 cup	almonds, soaked 12–48 hours
1 cup	pecans, soaked 1 hour
1	apple, shredded
½ cup	pitted dates
2 tablespoons	golden flaxseeds, ground
1 teaspoon	ground cinnamon
1 teaspoon	vanilla extract
½ teaspoon	Celtic salt

*P*rocess the almonds, pecans, apple, and dates through a Champion Juicer with the solid plate. Transfer to a bowl and stir in the flaxseeds, cinnamon, vanilla, and salt. Mix well.

Fruit Filling

8	fresh or dried strawberries
1½ tablespoons	water

*C*ombine the strawberries and water in a blender and process until smooth.

To assemble: Form the cookie dough into 1-inch balls. Using your thumb or index finger, make a depression in the center of each cookie. Fill the depression with some of the fruit filling. Place on a dehydrator sheet and dehydrate at 105 degrees for 8–10 hours or until the desired crispness is achieved.

Note: If the strawberries are not sweet enough, add a little stevia to taste. Any fresh or dried fruit may be used for the fruit filling.

Ice Cream and Sauces

Banana Ice Cream

Frozen bananas

Process frozen bananas through a Champion Juicer with the solid plate. Serve immediately.

Cosmic Strawberry Ice

yield: 3 ice cube trays (6–8 servings)

1 quart	Almond Milk (page 46)
2 cups	fresh strawberries

Combine the milk and strawberries in a blender and process until smooth. Pour into 3 ice cube trays and freeze 8 hours or overnight. When ready to serve, process the cubes through a Champion Juicer with the solid plate. Serve immediately.

Desserts

Divine Vanilla Ice

yield: 3 ice cube trays (6–8 servings)

1 quart	Almond Milk (page 46)
2 teaspoons	vanilla extract

Add the vanilla extract to the milk and stir well. Pour into 3 ice cube trays and freeze 8 hours or overnight. When ready to serve, process the cubes through a Champion Juicer with the solid plate. Serve immediately.

Heavenly Orange Sherbet

yield: 3 ice cube trays (6–8 servings)

1 quart	Almond Milk (page 46)
2 cups	fresh orange juice
2 teaspoons	vanilla extract

Combine all the ingredients in a blender and process until well mixed. Pour into 3 ice cube trays and freeze 8 hours or overnight. When ready to serve, process the cubes through a Champion Juicer with the solid plate. Serve immediately.

Raspberry Sauce

Fresh or frozen raspberries
Coconut water as needed

Place the raspberries in a blender and process until smooth. Add a small amount of coconut water as needed to achieve the desired consistency.

Strawberry Sauce

Fresh or frozen strawberries
Coconut water as needed

Place the strawberries in a blender and process until smooth. Add a small amount of coconut water as needed to achieve the desired consistency.

Desserts

Pies

Banana Crème Pie

yield: 6–8 servings

Crust

2 cups	pecans, soaked 1 hour
½ cup	pitted dates, soaked 1 hour

Place the pecans in a food processor fitted with the S blade and process into a fine meal. Gradually add the dates and continue processing until the dough forms a ball. Press into a 9-inch glass pie plate.

Banana Crème Pie (continued)

Filling

2 cups	young coconut pulp
2	ripe bananas
2 tablespoons	psyllium powder
	Young coconut water as needed

Combine the coconut pulp, bananas, and psyllium powder in a food processor fitted with the S blade, or in a blender, and process until smooth and creamy.

Decoration

2	ripe bananas, thinly sliced
1	strawberry for garnish
	Sprigs of fresh mint for garnish

To assemble: Arrange about two-thirds of the banana slices evenly over the bottom of the pie crust (reserve the remaining slices). Pour the filling over the banana slices. Arrange the remaining banana slices in a circle on top of the filling, place the strawberry in the center, and surround the strawberry with sprigs of fresh mint. Refrigerate for 2–3 hours before serving.

Desserts

Blueberry Crème Pie with Peach Filling

yield: 6–8 servings

Crust

2 cups	pecans, soaked 1 hour
2 cups	shredded dried coconut
¼ cup	pitted dates

*P*lace the pecans in a food processor fitted with the S blade and process into a fine meal. Gradually add the coconut and dates and continue processing until the dough forms a ball. Press into a 9-inch glass pie plate.

Filling

2 cups	young coconut pulp
1½ cups	fresh blueberries
½ cup	macadamia nuts, soaked 1 hour
¼ cup	pitted dates, soaked 1 hour
1 tablespoon	psyllium powder

Blueberry Crème Pie with Peach Filling
(continued)

Combine the coconut, blueberries, macadamia nuts, dates, and psyllium powder in a food processor fitted with the S blade, or in a blender, and process until smooth and creamy.

Decoration

> 2   ripe peaches, thinly sliced
>   Blueberries
>   Mint leaves for garnish

To assemble: Arrange about two-thirds of the peach slices evenly over the bottom of the pie crust. Pour the filling over the peach slices and top with the remaining peach slices and a few blueberries. Garnish with mint leaves. Refrigerate for 2–3 hours before serving.

Desserts

Carob Crème Pie

yield: 6–8 servings

Crust

2 cups	pecans, soaked 1 hour
½ cup	pitted honey dates or medjool dates

Place the pecans in a food processor fitted with the S blade and process into a fine meal. Gradually add the dates and continue processing until the dough forms a ball. Press into a 9-inch glass pie plate and place in a dehydrator for 2 hours at 105 degrees.

Filling

3 cups	young coconut pulp
½ cup	young coconut water
6 tablespoons	raw carob powder
1 tablespoon	psyllium powder
¼ teaspoon	Celtic salt

Combine all the ingredients in a blender and process until smooth. Pour into the prepared crust and refrigerate 2–3 hours before serving.

Variation: Arrange a layer of sliced bananas evenly over the bottom of the crust before pouring in the filling.

Peach Pie

Crust

2 cups	pecans, soaked 1 hour
½ cup	pitted dates

Place the pecans in a food processor fitted with the S blade and process into a fine meal. Gradually add the dates, and continue processing until the dough forms a ball. Press into a 9-inch glass pie plate.

Filling

6 large	ripe peaches
1 tablespoon	psyllium powder

Place 3 of the peaches in a blender and process until smooth and creamy. Add the psyllium and process until blended. Slice the remaining 3 peaches and arrange them evenly over the bottom of the prepared crust. Pour the filling over the sliced peaches. Refrigerate for 2–3 hours before serving.

Desserts

Delightful Raspberry Crème Pie

Crust

2 cups	pecans, soaked 1 hour
½ cup	pitted dates

*P*lace the pecans in a food processor fitted with the S blade and process into a fine meal. Gradually add the dates and continue processing until the dough forms a ball. Press into a 9-inch glass pie plate.

Filling

2 cups	almonds, soaked 12–48 hours and blanched (see page 34)
1 cup	young coconut pulp
	Young coconut water as needed
1 cup	fresh or frozen raspberries
2 teaspoons	vanilla extract

*C*ombine the almonds and coconut in a blender and process until smooth, thick, and creamy. Add just enough coconut water to facilitate blending. Add the raspberries and vanilla and process until smooth. Pour into the prepared crust and freeze until firm but not solidly frozen. Garnish the chilled pie with a few whole raspberries and mint leaves just before serving.

Strawberry Angel Crème Pie

yield: 6–8 servings

Crust

2 cups	pecans, soaked 1 hour
1 cup	pitted honey dates or medjool dates
2 teaspoons	ground cinnamon

Place the pecans in a food processor fitted with the S blade and process into a fine meal. Gradually add the dates and cinnamon and continue processing until the dough forms a ball. Press the dough into a 9-inch glass pie plate.

Filling

2 cups	strawberries
2 cups	young coconut pulp
¼ cup	pitted dates, soaked 15 minutes
1 tablespoon	psyllium powder
½ teaspoon	ground cinnamon

Combine all the ingredients in a blender and process until smooth. Pour the filling into the prepared crust. Refrigerate for 2–3 hours before serving. Garnish each serving with sliced strawberries and a mint leaf.

Desserts

Italian Crème Pie

Crust

2½ cups	pecans, soaked 1 hour
1¼ cups	pitted medjool dates

Place the pecans in a food processor fitted with the S blade and process into a fine meal. Gradually add the dates and continue processing until the dough forms a ball. Press into a 9-into glass pie plate.

Filling

1½ cups	almonds, soaked 12–48 hours and blanched (see page 34)
1 cup	water
3 large	ripe bananas
2½ teaspoons	vanilla extract
1¼ teaspoons	rum extract (add more for a stronger rum flavor)
¾ teaspoon	almond extract

Italian Crème Pie (continued)

Combine the almonds and water in a blender and process until smooth and creamy. Add the bananas and the extracts and continue blending until smooth. Pour into the prepared crust and freeze until firm but not solidly frozen.

Topping

1 cup	cashews, soaked 1 hour
2/3 cup	water
6 tablespoons	raw carob powder
4	pitted medjool dates

Combine all the ingredients in a food processor fitted with the S blade, or in a blender, and process until smooth and creamy.

Decoration

1	orange, very thinly sliced

To decorate: Garnish each serving with a dollop of the topping and an orange slice.

Mango Crème Pie

Crust

2 cups	almonds, soaked 12–48 hours, then dehydrated 18–24 hours at 105 degrees
2 cups	shredded dried coconut
¼ cup	pitted dates
1 tablespoon	coconut oil

Place the almonds in a food processor fitted with the S blade and process into a fine meal. Gradually add the coconut, dates, and coconut oil and process until well blended. Press into a 9-inch glass pie plate.

Filling

1½ cups	chopped ripe mango
1 cup	dried mango, soaked 1 hour
1 cup	young coconut pulp
1 tablespoon	psyllium powder
1 cup	sliced strawberries, or 1 ripe banana, sliced
	Mint leaves for garnish

Combine the fresh mango, dried mango, and coconut pulp in a food processor fitted with the S blade and process until smooth and creamy. Add the psyllium powder and mix well. Reserve a few strawberry slices for the garnish, and arrange the remaining slices evenly over the bottom of the prepared crust. Pour the filling over the strawberries. Refrigerate for 2–3 hours before serving. Garnish with the reserved strawberry slices and fresh mint leaves.

Tastes Like Pumpkin Pie

This recipe was in Living in the Raw.

Filling

4 cups	chopped carrots
1½ cups	pitted honey dates
¾ cup	almonds, soaked 12–48 hours and blanched (see page 34)
½ cup	walnuts, soaked 6 hours
2 teaspoons	ground cinnamon
1 teaspoon	ground ginger
1 teaspoon	vanilla extract
¼ teaspoon	ground cloves

Process the carrots, dates, almonds, and walnuts through a Champion Juicer with the solid plate. Stir in the cinnamon, ginger, vanilla, and cloves and mix well. Press into a 9- or 10-inch glass pie plate and refrigerate until firm.

Topping

1 cup	almonds, soaked 12–48 hours and blanched (see page 34)
½ cup	pitted honey dates
1 teaspoon	vanilla extract
1 teaspoon	shredded dried coconut

Process the almonds and dates through a Champion Juicer with the solid plate. Add the vanilla and enough water to obtain a creamy consistency. Using the flat side of a knife, spread the topping over the filling and sprinkle with the coconut. Chill thoroughly before serving.

Puddings

Carob Pudding

yield: 2–4 servings

2 cups	young coconut pulp
½ cup	pecans, soaked 1 hour
1–2 tablespoons	raw carob powder
1 teaspoon	vanilla extract
	Young coconut water or water as needed

Combine all the ingredients in a blender and process until smooth, thick, and creamy, adding just enough coconut water to facilitate blending. Refrigerate for 2 hours before serving.

Note: For extra sweetness, blend in stevia or a few soaked dates to taste.

Carob Fantasy Pudding

yield: 2–4 servings

2 cups	young coconut pulp
½ cup	macadamia nuts, soaked 1 hour
1–2 tablespoons	raw carob powder
2 teaspoons	vanilla extract
	Young coconut water as needed

Combine all the ingredients in a blender and process until smooth, thick, and creamy, adding just enough coconut water to facilitate blending. Refrigerate for 2 hours before serving.

Carob Mousse

yield: 2–4 servings

2 cups	young coconut pulp
1	ripe avocado
½ cup	raw carob powder
¼ cup	pine nuts, soaked 30 minutes
2 teaspoons	vanilla extract

Combine all the ingredients in a blender and process until smooth, thick, and creamy. Refrigerate for 2 hours before serving.

Note: For extra sweetness in either the Carob Fantasy Pudding or Carob Mousse, blend in stevia or a few soaked dates to taste.

Desserts

Coconut Cashew Pudding

yield: 2–4 servings

2 cups	young coconut pulp
1/2 cup	cashews, soaked 1 hour
1–2 tablespoons	raw carob powder
1 teaspoon	vanilla extract
	Young coconut water as needed

Combine all the ingredients in a blender and process until smooth, thick, and creamy, adding just enough coconut water to facilitate blending. Refrigerate for 2 hours before serving.

Coconut Pistachio Pudding

yield: 2–4 servings

2 cups	young coconut pulp
1 1/2 cups	young coconut water
1	ripe avocado
1/2 cup	raw pistachios, soaked 4–6 hours
1/2 cup	raisins, soaked 3–4 hours
2 teaspoons	vanilla extract

Combine all the ingredients in a blender and process until smooth, thick, and creamy. Refrigerate for 2 hours before serving.

Mango Pudding

yield: 4–6 servings

2 cups	chopped ripe mango
1 cup	young coconut pulp
¼ cup	young coconut water or water
1 teaspoon	psyllium powder
1 teaspoon	vanilla extract

Combine all the ingredients in a blender and process until smooth, thick, and creamy. Refrigerate for 2 hours before serving.

Mexican Carob Orange Pudding

yield: 2–4 servings

2 cups	young coconut pulp
1	orange
½ cup	almonds, soaked 12–48 hours
2–3 tablespoons	raw carob powder
2 teaspoons	vanilla extract

Combine all the ingredients in a blender and process until smooth, thick, and creamy. Refrigerate for 2 hours before serving.

Desserts

Mexican Rice Pudding

3 cups	young coconut pulp
1 cup	young coconut water
2 teaspoons	ground cinnamon, plus additional for garnish
2 teaspoons	vanilla extract
1 cup	wild rice, soaked 3–5 days (soak until soft)

Combine the coconut pulp, coconut water, cinnamon, and vanilla in a blender and process until smooth, thick, and creamy. Transfer to a bowl and stir in the rice. Mix well. Refrigerate for 2 hours before serving. Garnish each serving with a sprinkle of cinnamon, if desired.

Note: For extra sweetness, blend in soaked dates to taste with the coconut mixture. The dates should be soaked 15 minutes prior to blending.

Pineapple Parfait

yield: 2–4 servings

1½ cups	young coconut pulp
1½ cups	fresh or frozen pineapple
½ cup	macadamia nuts, soaked 1 hour
1 teaspoon	vanilla extract
	Young coconut water or water as needed
	Ripe bananas, sliced
	Fresh strawberries
	Mint leaves

Combine the coconut pulp, pineapple, macadamia nuts, and vanilla in a blender and process until smooth, thick, and creamy, adding just enough coconut water to facilitate blending. Refrigerate 2 hours before serving. Layer the pudding with sliced bananas in parfait glasses. Top each serving with a fresh strawberry and a mint leaf.

Desserts

Recommended Reading

Highest Recommendation:

Cousens, Gabriel. *Conscious Eating*. Berkeley, CA: North Atlantic Books, 2000.

Additional Reading:

Anderson, Richard. *Cleanse and Purify Thyself*, Book Series. Medford, OR: Christobe Publishing, 2000.

Cousens, Gabriel. *Spiritual Nutrition and the Rainbow Diet*. Boulder, CO: Cassandra Press, 1987.

Meyerowitz, Steve. *Food Combining and Digestion*. Great Barrington, MA: Sproutman Publications, 2002.

Meyerowitz, Steve. *Juice Fasting and Detoxification*. Great Barrington, MA: Sproutman Publications, 1999.

Meyerowitz, Steve. *Sprouts The Miracle Food*. Great Barrington, MA: Sproutman Publications, 1998.

Meyerowitz, Steve. *Wheatgrass Nature's Finest Medicine*. Great Barrington, MA: Sproutman Publications, 1999.

Rodwell, Julie, ed. *The Complete Book of Raw Food*, Long Island, NY: Hatherleigh Press, 2003.

Wolfe, David. *Eating for Beauty*. San Diego: Maul Brothers Publishing, 2002.

Wolfe, David. *Sunfood Diet Success System*. San Diego: Maul Brothers Publishing, 2000.

Young, Robert O., and Shelley Redford Young. *The pH Miracle*. New York: Warner Books, 2002.

Resource Guide

Adams Olive Ranch
19401 Road 220
Strathmore, CA 93267
Phone: 888-216-5483
Web site: www.AdamsOliveRanch.com
Raw organic olives.

Anderson's Almonds
6401 Hultberg Road
Hilmar, CA 95324
Phone: 209-667-7494
Email: info@andersonalmonds.com
Web site: www.andersonalmonds.com
Organic almonds (very good prices).

Bariani Olive Oil Company
9460 Bar Du Lane
Sacramento, CA 95829
Phone: 415-864-1917
Email: info@barianioliveoil.com
Web site: www.barianioliveoil.com
High quality olive oil (the best; this is the olive oil I use).

Barleans Organic Oils
4936 Lake Terrell Road
Ferndale, WA 98248
Phone: 800-445-3529
Web site: www.barleans.com
High-quality organic oils.

Big Tree Organics
PMB 102
Turlock, CA 95324
Phone: 209-669-3678
Email: info@bigtreeorganic.com
Web site: www.bigtreeorganic.com
Organic almonds (excellent prices).

Diamond Organics
1272 Highway 1
Moss Landing, CA 95079
Phone: 888-674-2642
Web site: www.diamondorganics.com
Organic produce delivered, sprouting supplies, dehydrated foods, and desserts.

Flora Inc.
PO Box 73
Lynden, WA 98264
Phone: 800-446-2110
Web site: www.florahealth.com
High quality organic oils.

Frontier Natural Products
PO Box 299
Norway, IA 52318
Phone: 800-669-3275
Web site: www.frontiercoop.com
Dried herbs, spices, extracts, aromatherapy oils, and natural skin care products.

Goldmine Natural Foods
7805 Arjons Drive, Suite B
San Diego, CA 92126-4368
Phone: 800-475-3663
Web site: www.goldminenaturalfood.com
Sea vegetables.

Jaffe Brothers
28560 Lilac Road
Valley Center, CA 92082
Phone: 760-746-1133
Web site: www.organicfruitsandnuts.com
Organic nuts and seeds.

Living Tree Community
PO Box 10082
Berkeley, CA 98248
Phone: 800-260-5534
Web site: www.livingtreecommunity.com
Nuts, seeds, and nut butters.

Maine Coast Sea Vegetables
RR 1 Box 78
Franklin, ME 04634-9708
Web site: www.seaveg.com
Sea vegetables.

Manitoba Harvest
#15-2166 Notre Dame Avenue
Winnipeg, Manitoba
Canada R3H OK2
Phone: 800-665-HEMP
Web site: www.manitobaharvest.com
Hemp nuts, hemp butter, protein powder, oils.

Morningstarr
Rose Lee Calabro, author
PO Box 465
Boulder Creek, CA 95006
Phone: 877-557-4711
Email: livingintheraw1@hotmail.com or livingintheraw@netzero.net
Web site: www.livingintheraw.com
Books; equipment; consultations on food preparation and setting up a raw food kitchen.

Nature's First Law
Phone: 800-205-2350
Web site: www.rawfood.com
Superstore of books, videos, equipment, and organic food.

New Natives
PO Box 1413
Freedom, CA 95019
Phone: 831-728-4136
Web site: www.newnatives.com
Organic sprouts, wheatgrass, supplies.

Nutiva
PO Box 1716
Sebastopol, CA 95473
Phone: 800-993-4367
Web site: www.nutiva.com
Organic hemp nuts, hemp oil, coconut oil,
and protein powder.

Omega Nutrition
6515 Aldrich Road
Bellingham, WA 98226
Phone: 800-661-3529
Web site: www.omegaflo.com
High quality organic oils.

Pure Joy Living Foods
Phone: 831-423-4557
Web site: www.purejoylivingfoods.com
Amazing nut milk bag.

Redmond Minerals, Inc.
Redmond, UT 84652
Phone: 800-367-7258
Web site: www.realsalt.com
RealSalt (highly recommended; I use this).

Rejuvenative Foods
PO Box 8464
Santa Cruz, CA 95060
Phone: 831-457-2418
Web site: www.rejuvenative.com
Nut butters and sauerkraut.

Sprout House
Phone: 800-SPROUTS (777-6887)
Email: info@sprouthouse.com
Web site: www.sprouthouse.com
Organic sprouting seeds, hemp sprouting
bags, raw food books, and Kitchen Garden
Salad Grower Sprouting Kit.

SunOrganic Farm
PO Box 409
San Marcos, CA 92079
Phone: 888-269-9888
Web site: www.sunorganic.com
Organic nuts, seeds, dates, sprouting supplies.

About the Author

Rose Lee Calabro is the author of *Living in the Raw* and has also contributed recipes to *The Complete Book of Raw Foods*. Rose Lee has traveled all over the country lecturing and teaching living and raw food classes. She discovered living and raw food over nine years ago in a class given by Pam Masters (*Living in the Raw* is dedicated to Pam). In a very short time she began to have more energy and lost a great deal of weight, and her body began to heal very quickly.

Rose Lee has dedicated her life to teaching about living and raw food and inspiring and motivating people to make positive changes in their lives.

Index

BOOK PUBLISHING COMPANY

since 1974—books that educate, inspire, and empower

To find your favorite vegetarian and soyfood products online, visit:

www.healthy-eating.com

Living in the Raw
Rose Lee Calabro
1-57067-148-6 $19.95

Raw Food Made Easy
Jenny Cornbleet
1-57067-175-3 $16.95

Warming Up to
Living Foods
Elysa Markowitz
1-57067-065-X $15.95

Smoothie Power
Robert Oser
1-57067-177-X $9.95

Sea Vegetable Celebration
Shep Erhart & Leslie Cerier
1-57067-123-0 $14.95

Juice Power
Teoorah B.N. Shaleahk
1-57067-168-0 $9.95

Purchase these health titles and cookbooks from your local bookstore or
natural food store, or you can buy them directly from:
Book Publishing Company • P.O. Box 99 • Summertown, TN 38483
1-800-695-2241

Please include $3.95 per book for shipping and handling.